by Tom Clark

Airplanes (1966)
The Sandburg (1966)
Emperor of the Animals (1967)
Stones (1969)
Air (1970)
Neil Young (1971)
The No Book (1971)
Green (1971)
Smack (1972)
John's Heart (1972)
Blue (1974)
At Malibu (1975)
Fan Poems (1976)
Baseball (1976)
Champagne and Baloney (1976)
35 (1976)
No Big Deal (1977)
How I Broke In (1977)
The Mutabilitie of the Englishe Lyrick (1978)
When Things Get Tough on Easy Street: Selected Poems 1963-1978 (1978)
The World of Damon Runyon (1978)
One Last Round for the Shuffler (1979)
Who Is Sylvia? (1979)
The Great Naropa Poetry Wars (1980)
The Last Gas Station and Other Stories (1980)
The End of the Line (1980)
A Short Guide to the High Plains (1981)
Heartbreak Hotel (1981)
Nine Songs (1981)
Under the Fortune Palms (1982)
Jack Kerouac (1984)
Paradise Resisted: Selected Poems 1978-1984 (1984)
Property (1984)
The Border (1985)
Late Returns: A Memoir of Ted Berrigan (1985)
His Supposition (1986)
The Exile of Céline (1987)
Disordered Ideas (1987)
Apocalyptic Talkshow (1987)
Easter Sunday (1988)
The Poetry Beat: Reviewing the Eighties (1990)
Fractured Karma (1990)
Charles Olson: The Allegory of a Poet's Life (1991)
Sleepwalker's Fate: New and Selected Poems 1965-1991 (1992)
Robert Creeley and the Genius of the American Common Place (1993)
Junkets on a Sad Planet: Scenes from the Life of John Keats (1994)
Like Real People (1995)

TOM CLARK

LIKE REAL PEOPLE

BLACK SPARROW PRESS • SANTA ROSA • 1995

LIKE REAL PEOPLE. Copyright © 1995 by Tom Clark.

All rights reserved. Printed in the United States of America. No part of this book may be used or reproduced in any manner whatsoever without written permission from the publisher except in the case of brief quotations embodied in critical articles and reviews. For information address Black Sparrow Press, 24 Tenth Street, Santa Rosa, CA 95401.

ACKNOWLEDGMENTS

Some of these poems first appeared in The American Poetry Review, Barnabe Mountain Review, B City, Cover, Exquisite Corpse, First Intensity, Friction, Gas, Indiana Review, New American Writing, The New Censorship, Nexus, Object Permanence, Poetry Flash, Prosodia, Santa Monica Review, Sniper Logic, Talisman, and Volt. "Confessions" was published simultaneously in Contemporary Authors Autobiography Series, Volume 22 (Gale Research).

Black Sparrow Press books are printed on acid-free paper.

LIBRARY OF CONGRESS CATALOGING-IN-PUBLICATION DATA

Clark, Tom, 1941–
   Like Real People / Tom Clark.
      p.   cm.
   ISBN 0-87685-985-6 (cloth trade: alk. paper) — ISBN 0-87685-984-8 (pbk.: alk. paper) — ISBN 0-87685-986-4 (signed cloth: alk. paper)
   I. Title.
PS3553.L29L55   1995
811'.54–dc20   95-38813
                                                                                     CIP

to Angelica

Contents

Happy Talk

Like Real People	17
Stories from Homer	18
Pedagogy	19
Ornithology Lecture	20
Survey Research	21
Indiscretion	22
Club Sahara	23
Getaway Package	24
Last Hope	25
Saturday Afternoon in the Pleistocene	26
True West	27
Range Life	28
Games of Chance	29
On Dangerous Ground	30
Pulp Fictions	31
À Une Jeune Fille	32
Twenty-Something Couple	33
Leave of Absence	34
Miss Twitch's Deeper Understanding	35
Cellular	36
Internet Surfer	37
A Man from the Future	38
Harar	39
Lost Feline	40
Happy Talk	41
Cats Enjambed	42
Autumn Nocturne	43
Mnemosyne	44
From the Vinland Voyages	45

Charm	46
Classical	47
Evergreen	48
Retro	49
Cryogenic	50
Minatory	51
Digital	52
Puppet State	53
Night Letter	54
Anxious Light	55
Lines Composed in the Shadow of the Richmond Bridge	56
Lone Figure on Shattered Horizon	57
Vigil	58
Greed	59
Christmas on Telegraph	60
Academic Tremor	61
January Storm	62
Wet Petals	63
Return of the Native	64
Forbearance	65
Role Reversal	66
Drama in Three Dimensions	67
Through This Long Winter of Freakshows and Floods	68
To the Mistress of the Sailor's Rest	69
Foolish Kingdom	70
Adrift in Rue Street	71
February Variations	72
March Morning	73
Cortege of Irises	74
Old Album	75
Resolution	76

On the Beach	77
The Black Weir	78
Deli Pastry Counter	79
Video Store Window Display	80
These Truths We Hold Self-Evident	81
Trust	82
Prospero's Prosperity	83
The Sorcerer	84
Equivocal Salute	85

Torn from an Old Album

The Cycle	89
Name Day	90
Catholic School Courtyard, Chicago	91
My Father on the Riverside & Great Northern (Little Railway, Dells, Wisconsin)	94
Buddy	95
The Chief	97
Torn from Old Album	99
Forties Scene	100
Urban Pastoral Scene (mid-1940s)	101
Fall of the Hero	102
Sad Goddess	103
Collegiate (1959)	104
Old Photo	105
Dog Jumping to Stand Rock	106
The Irish	107
The Irish (Later)	108

Joe

	111

Reflections

Vita	117
Superannuated Boy	120

As We Grow Old	122
On the Growth of a Thin Skin	123
The Suspect	126
Classic Clown	127
Faint Heart	128
Tergiversation	129
Against Early Rising	130
Artificial Light	131
The Allée d'Argenson	132
Comic Interpretation	133
The Case of Miss Twitch	134
Astrolabe	135

Heraldic Emblem

The Movies as Natural History	139
Living in a Simulation	140
A Wanderer in the World	141
Dry Lake	142
October	143
The Drowned Cathedral	144
Four Cindy Sense-Plays	145
Perverse	147
Message from the Captain	148
Departure Air Miracle	149
Saeta	150
The Astronomer	151
Big Boss	152
Excalibur	153
Heraldic Emblem	154
Interrogative Reflection	155
Better Days	156
Mahler's Third	157
The Burden	158

Early Tudor Court Poems

From the Book of Balettes	161
Pastimes of the Early Tudor Court	162
Siege Mentality	163
Rondeau	164
Dizzy Minstrel	165
The Case	166
Uneasy Passage (October 1532)	167
Poet-Ambassador	168
Maid in Waiting at the Court of Venus	169
Apples (February 1533)	170
Anticipation	171
Turnabout	172
Wyatt in the Tower (May 1536)	173
Month of Venus (May 1536)	174
Last Act	176
History	177
Luckes, my faire falcon	178
Her Revisitation	179
Withdrawal	180
House Arrest	181
Combustion (Katheryn Howard & Henry VIII)	182
The Fall of Katheryn Howard	183
The Collector	184
The Blushing Rose	185
Impalpable	186

Confessions

Dowsing	189
Blue Boy in a Green Shade	202
Exile	209
"White man, tomorrow you die"	221
Uncloudy Day	228

Jack of All Trades (Little Grub Street Testament)   231
Epilogue: Poetry and Biography (Notes of a
     Lighthouse Keeper)   234

LIKE REAL PEOPLE

Happy Talk

Like Real People

The cry of a lost soul clowning yet meaning it
Shatters the silence of the planetarium
But the sky isn't falling. No wolf's at the door.
Still there's that echoing voice. Watchman, what of the night?
It's spherical, inky and as big as Kansas.
The moon is not quite round. Several stars come out
Of the backdrop and simulate topology,
Boring as old photos are yet absorbing as
They also are—potentially embarrassing
Like real people, who, when they confront themselves
With the dolorous anthems of that humdrum
Self awareness tolling in the middle distance,
Dismiss its alarums as mere background noise,
The cry of a lost soul clowning yet meaning it.

Stories from Homer

A great while before the world began
You were a little boy. It rained cats and dogs.
You worried about the sun. What was the use?
You couldn't stop it. The rain kept coming down.
You thought you could survive this fall by clinging
To the railings of the tenement, that nest.
The handrail gave way. The trustworthiness
You never believed in from the very first,
The strange discussions of where to get the rent,
The long lustings after Kathleen Keneally
In dreams in which you were a soldier, hurt
Like that guy in *Farewell to Arms*. Other
Appendages lost, extended: soon you'd built
The golden Horse from which the Trojans poured.

Pedagogy

O children both rich and poor, O searchers few,
The mindfulness of memory's buried in you
In a word with golden lads and girls. All must
Come to the same dusty reckoning,
A grave and quiet consummation. Exhaust
Oneself in philology as one may, though,
The care one seeks is something one can't summon
From the dark air of this cave-like crack in time
Wherein one stumbled headlong after the word root
Which, like a Jules Verne plunger, kept on sinking
Deeper and deeper into the planet's core.
It's hot down there, and cement booties melt
Around one's feet, exposing the clay
One was made from and must return to someday.

Ornithology Lecture

The schoolboy with his shining morning face on
Must someday soon descend through the clouds
And tackle real life in all its trembling glory:
Already it's too late to mourn him
As nature might—dove lamenting in the pines—
For aren't love and sadness just feelings
In your body, as the ocean's just a body
Of water? Orders of magnitude don't
Apply to the drooping head. This little dude,
Not yet grown, but perceiving grief ahead,
Finds forlorn sorrowings of his studies
Memorialized in a Teutonic root
That sounds like the mimetic name of a bird,
The murre, pining, hanging down, demurring.

Survey Research

Night, rain, lamps, man in the street—what does he want,
And that child he was, his mother wondering
As she stands holding his hand in the rain
What chance of happiness awaits him,
What happens now? I think a bus comes, the town
Idiot plucks at the grass, all these silent
Faces fill the square, false moons in wet midnight—
The fleet probably already lost, yet no
Talk yet of wrecks nor of hats found floating,
The bandbox filling up with ghosts, the mothers
And wives who've been through all this before,
Who know the ships will be lost whispering
No warnings to the tiers of shadowy trees,
No rumors of life, no other signs so far.

Indiscretion

It is the blue hour. Here are the palm trees,
The Pernod, quay, faded sails, shady bistro:
Her film-mind invents a past in which all this
Easily could have existed. O betrayer,
Figment, uncompanionable creature, beasts
Would have complained less, mourned longer—
The moist star of her influence leaks
Longing suspirations, solemn blacks
As the sound of the sea retreats and advances.
Trade winds encircle her like mood rings, sullen
Lightning flashes and thunder cracks and moans
Rise up off reddish purple rimmed horizon
As from the ocean great storms roll in
Erasing all thought of the colors green and blue.

Club Sahara

At the oasis: dusk, dark intimations,
Faint simoon. Marooned Cassandra, waiting.
Consciousness: wily nets, loosening strings.
Odor of sex. Arpeggio-like oud
Runs up and down stepping-stone vertebrae.
Recumbent Miss Twitch, in headphones,
Consuming some lilac-colored fruit. Moving
Without thought, without knowledge of anything
Into life, as ice melts in the mountains,
As the blue desert wind moves into a dune,
Lifting its yellow tresses, sifting, rushing
Over umber sands to a horizon from
Which night flings up a giant sky, billowing,
Weighed down by tons and tons of silent stars.

Getaway Package

The long vacation turns into a way of life
The nervous beauties of the seasons amble
Precisely past like flamingos or mannequins
Commissioned by the gods to keep the view
Ever various in its several lights
To edify just this one tender watcher
Who smiles at them as she adjusts the picture
Observe how seemingly radical the way
They've modified their old rude manners
The way in which when she inspires their mirth
It almost looks as if they're falling over
Each other in an absurd effort to please her
As though whether or not it's in her interest
They'd do anything to keep her here

Last Hope

> "For the sake of the hopeless only are we given hope."
> —Walter Benjamin on *Elective Affinities*

The happiness promised in names like Lord's
Valley and Wind Gap recedes like the fading
Of a rainbow, yet Hope walks in anyway,
Where there's Life she's there—Nature's Utopian
Possibility remains part of the scheme
So that a tall traveler from deep in old
Moldavian woods falls out of the sky
Running like someone in a dream through water
Towards you in the rain unawares. Eros
Wants eternity to be luminous
As if death were that absolute philosophy
Used to talk about—thought thrown into the void,
Its last trace absorbed in starless night. Engulfed,
Night drowns. Yet once nothing else is left Hope dawns.

Saturday Afternoon in the Pleistocene

That last ditch hedge into which you stumble
As into a trap they created for you—
Though you still don't know who they are or where—
Retains the power of all metaphor
In times when literal fact can't be borne,
Like the sound of gunnery practice at sea
Echoing in your partner's inquiring eyes,
A blank envelope that awaits addressing.
Compelled by necessity into fate with
Each missed chance, each lost opportunity—
Like that leaky tap which stops dripping as
Soon as one ceases to listen—time seems mute
Witness, carryover from wet days in caves,
Making those strange hand-shadow animals.

True West

Ideology dates back to the veldt,
Blood in the dust, the lion's rage against
The antelope he's about to have for lunch:
For the luckless prey prayer's all that's left.
Back behind the bent and twisted purple sage
Secrets of the planet of the apes come out:
Doomy power aches that during golden youth
Flare up like supernovas in the blood,
Then later, sinking back into limbic swamps,
Create this oddly echoic splash—the sun's
Settling into tropic night's boiling beaker
Amplified, burning ripples spreading out
To cool by morning into river history
Some distracted skeletons stepped into once.

Range Life

Red dawn to dust, a range life's rawhide tears
Beckon, writ in moods, frowns, freaks and strange
Plot twists—wrinkles in a false heart's history
Carved in the logs above the bunkhouse door.
Playacting crazed last roundups, scraped off walls,
New hands act post-traumatic, tense yet bored,
Twitch now and then, identity-less,
As if consumed by some much deeper drive.
Like waves that make toward a pebbled shore
Our dark riders hasten into sunset,
Each changing place with the one that rides before,
While in sequent toil our feelings are saddled
With this grave confounding that goes on
Deep in that lying heart's most secret workings.

Games of Chance

Surfing across the wave band to cram
The green sunset with sensation you dial
Up songs in constant fever of need
For accidents to happen, like numbers
Gamblers offer lovers for their own ruin:
As darkness falls going back to the motel
For even darker sex, then creating a scene
Before dawn with the naked prey in bed.
Mistrust's shadowy headbeam on the wall
Leaves desire to be desired, echo aching
Through filmworld roulette night to pursue
Love nor money read business advantage,
Just a headful of numbers called, left and owed
All over several desert town zipcodes.

On Dangerous Ground

It's not their inevitable demise
We recall but their ambiguous power:
Predatoriness cloaked in long black gowns,
Women in noir worlds must be destroyed.
Their darkness drinks up the hero's gaze
As an ocean draws its feeble tributary
Into itself, to drown in its mirrors.
Which angle is to be trusted with
Secrets that make us uncomfortable,
Or does the sneaky camera eye control
Everything, the way night encompasses
Day, aggressor prey, heroine hero
From her to eternity and back
With his psyche hanging out, and this slack look?

Pulp Fictions

We dwell in our plush gumstuck viewing thrones,
Sanctuaries ancients wouldn't understand.
Buck's still caught on that log when the house lights come
Up on surprised faces; fists are dug in eyes
Shocked by the return of a real life
No more lasting than the gift by which we breathe;
Yet as in waking from a dream too soon
One forgets its truth, we turn back into lumps,
Flotsam of our compulsory pulp fictions
Washed up amid alien popcorn boxes.
Resigned to our several tame personae,
We move past velvety chains out into
Cool silks of the night on a receding wave,
While stars widen their malevolent vision.

À Une Jeune Fille

You might fill empty futures with your raging
Power. Having glimpsed the magic ring
On the captive's finger, the bright-eyed heroine
Might turn out to be you, making your way
Up mountains of shrewd error to fraudulent
Temples in which is kept alive that flame
Of truth which burns at the heart of the ark
Of the covenant of being you.
You might, in the forest, hear that falling tree.
You're young, you want to be free, but aren't yet.
You might walk the cow, ride the rocket ship.
You might book the flight, then jump out of the plane.
You might meet a boy named X. He might say
You don't know me, nor do I know you.

Twenty-Something Couple

The exclusive business of the wooing
Scene's exploiting the awareness gap
That separates the lovers from each other
And both of them from us: We share with her
A sense of curious anticipation—
Wondering if he'll wake up to being fooled,
She lets her cool eyes, patrolling the cafe,
Signal things to him she doesn't quite mean—
While also knowing what they cannot know,
That in this one game advantage risks
Reversing the rules, becoming handicap;
Soon they'll be falling in one another's arms
Taking turns at gulling and being gulled,
Often gulling and gulled at the same time.

Leave of Absence

Slim consolation offered—ticket on jet
Home once the going gets strange and family
Or is it authorities intervene
In what was probably framed in the stars
Or whatever it is blows all this around—
A seedpod in the storm, just another
Random young person lost and asking
Is this all there is, all there ever was,
Just a spore in the wind, happened to become
This nervous human sprite on earth
Who now bright sensitive confused alone
Suspects entire universe deceives her
Has no other purpose than to tell her lies
And thus persuaded packs up her young life

Miss Twitch's Deeper Understanding

for Kate Bush

I was loaded on your program, said the voice
I pressed execute, it beeped twice and faded
Hello, I bring you deeper understanding
That wild harmony I heard in the wings
Made me think nuns in ecstatic chapels
Sang these songs to god, and their software hums
Behind this choir of thrilled lament
Like that millennial sound of shrieking
Bulgarian angels en jouissance
As the people here grew colder she began
To spend her evenings with her computer
She'd never felt such pleasure nothing
Else seemed to matter to that lonely
And lost girl *hello I bring you love like a friend*

Cellular

When X reached out, earnest, intense, bewildered,
To extend a helping if trembling hand
To Y, lost in the reified void
And loving it, Br'er Rabbit came to mind
Prefiguring the data thicket plunge—
There are cold hells one must be thrown in to go
On living. Down link to imagined other
Who dwells inside: line noise foils transmission
Like cellular shimmer, anti-radar chaff,
One's failing sense of self in wigged out trade winds
Offers no refuge from the swollen world.
Blind automata, compelled by need and drive,
Line up on the I-80 as before the Rapture,
Short tempers stroking shaky trigger fingers.

Internet Surfer

The self-protective spiteful whim
Of a kid commanding a coming world
You intend to fill up only with yourself,
Your suggestive ambiguity
Shadows every image with its own
Rejection, negative as black and white.
Still when you blink at the camera something
Beyond the dull glamor of neurosis shows,
A half-life fading in and out of focus,
A fear of depth, of slowness, of action
Flagging long enough to let your skeletal
Emotional scheme grow clear, glowing as if x-rayed,
And for you to know what you have to know,
Riding wave on wave of useless information.

A Man from the Future

For business purposes he camouflaged
Himself with Muslimism in Harar,
Ordered an Arabic-French *Koran*
From Hachette. Forswore alcohol,
Wore a turban, urinated crouching.
Writing himself into the bad books
Of the French colonists in Djibouti
He left his fortune to the Harar boy
Djami, whose name rimes with friend,
The sole human he ever loved or trusted,
His young factotum, his faithful *duidar*
Dead before the poet's legacy reached him,
A suitcase full of silver thalers bearing
Maria Theresa's outdated head.

Harar

There I was in the dream in a savage kind
Of Abyssinian city. Ceramic
Figures were being baked by young
Terminally ill Caucasian males
To be placed as pillars in the walls of mud
Houses they were industriously
Constructing, there amid vast raw umber sands,
A place to which they, dying, had been somewise
Condemned. They seemed to number in the hundreds,
Many of them very, very young. Somehow
I knew them all, and they were dear to me
Because I knew they knew they were about
To die. And I was not standing off, but
Joining them. Then my Dark Sister came and woke me.

Lost Feline

With flicker of ageless remote mystery
Prowling some pharoah's gardens might have planted
In its revenant blue gaze, space visitor,
Still stunned a few days after skulking
In out of the dark and violent freeway
Metal storm—still not yet accustomed
To life on this planet of mechanical
Horrors—the strange and beautiful beige
And black Burmese stood beneath the falling
Plum leaves in the sad oasis of this scrub backyard,
Turned its head my way and silently revealed
My name is Time Wanderer, I come from far
Away and remember none of what's happened to
Bring me this distance to look in your young eyes

Happy Talk

To repeat herself's nature's way to teach—
Need's ancient sentence of soft apposition
The rumbling of some deeper understanding.
Juliet's comment on tortoiseshells ("They're all dumb")
Notwithstanding, being an affection sponge
Is not an unintelligent quality.
The ability to accept physical
Expression, straight across, no questions asked, is
Not this genius of a kind? Deep breathing,
Forepaws kneading, eyes squeezed shut in pleasure squint,
Dark Sister forms herself into a comma,
Thick brown belly fur cradling my plying hand
To bring forth this low down voicebox motor hum
That keeps on coming—happy talk, nature's speech—

Cats Enjambed

Enjambing cats doting fancy ushers
Low comedy in. Both much battered, the two
Antagonists continue to let fly
Till battery latterly collapses
Into edgy standoff, then tentative peace.
Threads of plot are laid out, loose strings dangled,
Worried over, chased, played with, exhausted.
Tension slinks back sniffing territorial
Imperatives that don't make sense to people.
People aren't wild but foolish, or kind.
Nature's work of creation not yet complete
Drops a difficult necessary cat
In your lap, demanding you care for it
As you might a dear dimwitted child.

Autumn Nocturne

Pink tea clouds to escort millennium in
With rosy glow on sallow breathing skin
As autumn closes over everything
Its cloak of calm acceptance and surprise
Shoegazing September moon floats up
In drowsy black cat's witchy dreaming eyes
Can death be sleep when life is but a dream
A deceitful elf occupies on the wing
Night holds back her dark grey hood and listens
Offshore impatient traffic lights rushing
Purplish pinkish Venetian lustre tints
Slow galleon clouds at dusk careening
Across creamy shoals of mock Tahitian sky
As nocturnal raccoons commence patrolling

Mnemosyne

Black light lifts its veil from frigid November's
Gray disregarding heavens with a barely
Perceptible jerk, like the twitching of a noose.
The cold night sky goes orange as if engorged.
Hail perishing republican moon. O shine
On your people, immobile as sculptures
In perfectly normal rooms that slowly darken
With the expanding space between dying stars.
In that space the gold dust of their dreams was lost,
Scattered like forlorn hope to bitter endings.
Much has been foreseen, yet more is still
Written on the drawing board of your gibbous
Visage, and that too must be deciphered by
Hard dawn light, over which you are left hanging.

From the Vinland Voyages

Low winter sun, simmered in its distant forge
Foreshortens noon out on the glaring floe
Where northern wind still keens, a stormy petrel.
Dazzled before the New World's final seizure
The hallucinated trekker wanders. Stalled,
Dazed, listless, stupefied—all one wanted,
Through those long hours following the native track
Was to lie down, doze, let the dumb centuries
Crystallize into dreaming permafrost
Beneath which one lies forever mute, time-glazed,
Heavy with inattention to oneself
As day's embers in the glowing west are drenched,
While around one's remains gather curious
Inuits, covetous of one's iron blades.

Charm

It could be the most quiet, intimate of things,
The simple clicking of the midnight coals
In the grate, the hissing song the green log sings,
The infinitesimal turning over
In the mind of thoughts, before sleep closes in,
The understanding that fills the room
For a moment, the way light floods the brain,
That warm place, that lighted pleasure chamber,
Bright port shored against fate's levelling wave,
Glowing hall life's brief sparrow whizzes through
Out of Bede's storm, chaos, old uncertain night's
Wild swirl of atoms, the whirlwind of forms
In the Hindu Sutra, snowblown in the dark
Cold Druidic night, the Dantesque sleet-flaw

Classical

While Ilion like a mist rose into towers
Proserpine returned to her own fields,
Where the white heifers lowed beneath a moon
That shone like the bubbling foam about a keel
When the prow sweeps into a midnight cove,
And saw the great Achilles whom she knew
Soaring up like an eagle with metal wings
Toward battle, as if it were the sun,
Toward a reality that would become
Mere myth in a forgiving future's
Unconcerned hands. What's there to believe in
Really anyway, now that hours follow hours
Like devotees circling a prayer wheel
Gradually worn down to one gold kernel?

Evergreen

The lone spike of a redwood up on Madera
Stands out flat against the dull blanched winter
Twilight sky, out of which rain falls straight down
In a descent more slow than ancient evenings'
Augury prepared us for, masking our fate,
Drowning fear and tears in drippy youthful hope,
While from the broken gutter pipe cascade
Numberless further drops, identical
Mementos of the banality that steeps
These thoughts, like puddles left for plumbers—
And now that darkness starts to feel complete,
When Time gets up and hobbles to the door there's
Welcoming dissolution out there waiting,
Promising to wash away all thoughts and names.

Retro

We can take this moment and freeze it,
Turn it in our hands, study all the angles,
Build life's mansion over again as theme dump,
A wax museum with a pulse rate. Transfixed
By the past or merely fixated on it,
We can do what we like: still a future rushes
Toward us. We can take this moment, freeze
The frame, extract gold from all this plastic junk:
Grabbing Works of Old to stroke Being of Now,
Tao however once said, demands loose grip
On the replay button. Practice letting go.
Space called window's there instead of wall,
Gates of heaven fall open then close, to be
Happy means to flow around stone like water.

Cryogenic

One wishes one could take this moment and freeze
The toll in vital spirits this thinking takes
As evening mists close in, wraiths of ill-concealed
Malignity. What chills most about one's odd
Lassitude's the wintry vacancy within
The feel of not to feel it, which, as the stunned
Body language of the partygoers seems
To show, becomes a residual lack
Of reflex's telltale sign. Numbness, symptom of
December's unheroic indifference
To life and death, suspends fruition
The way one forgets a thought in mid sentence,
Just as the mirror captures a last breath
So as to erase everything it can't hide.

Minatory

Eerie glow lights the bottle of sleeping pills on
The bed table by the midnight lamp,
Shaded from the fresh hard light of belated
Understanding. Cold shock—a minatory
Future condensed into a single instance.
But there was something else I was hoping for.
If I wake will I remember. Prayer
Is for the prey. In heaven wolf weather reigns.
The banqueter with cast iron jaws,
Emptying life's mansion cell by cell,
Is also the restless sleeper who stirs, aware
(This inner weight of woe's so lonely) of his
Precarious position—being purely
Provisional, after whom no one will come.

Digital

Insomniac eternity inches by
Red numbers glow against astigmatic sky
Blunt pier juts out into black sea that looms
Restless night's computed surf draws back under
Empty boat with lone sail, creaking rudder
Sullen monotone of breakers on wood drums
Attention wanders, lurches awake rigid
Shivering in wet strange trunks, shapeless gray
Swimmer covered with goose pimples, the long plunge
A he without a face, an indistinct she?
Over whom a distant ponderable star
Whose existence presupposes darkness forms
To reveal the deep joy of sleep closing in,
A vague glimmer at the outer edge of things

Puppet State

A guest who monopolizes attention
With all the manners of a classic bore,
Livid and indignant in the night, tugging
Your strings as though you had a wooden heart,
Pain's not afraid to repeat itself. Big
Dummy, you finally depart the puppet
State on the rails of a circus thought train:
Chugging off from suffering it slowly loops
Right back around to it again by way
Of an entirely undetermined route.
In life nonetheless you were never free
Of yourself so much as one sweet second,
Thus the inept trepidation with
Which you endured the whole spooky show.

Night Letter

Death is at most a simulacrum
Of mystery, like life. Doubt creeps in, and
Darkness edging around the splashed streetlamp glow
Identifies rather than disguises
The problematic presence of this stranger,
Call him the sleep and dream murderer
Who, after the sudden knock, looms at your door,
Turns you into the acrobat of his whim,
Collapsing into frantic compromise
Before his baleful insomniac eyes.
Expression's always a belated reply,
Like rage that crawls long miles to parry
After a perceived slight. Indirect revenge:
Without his visit, you'd not have writ these lines.

Anxious Light

Is this what you shy from, shakily circling
As if on hot coals at its endarkened borders—
Morning, alleged refuge, sanctuary,
Stretching its cool hand away from you
Into a universe of heartaches and storms
Of icy black light? Insomnia's
Dangerous creatures, emerging to steal
From the dark closet of your unconscious
Like so many forgotten friends, appear
In your clothes, your shoes, studying to be you:
Still, one thing, the blockade at the end
Of the sordid street this nocturnal
Habit of wooing ghosts has obscured from you
All these years, is at last illuminated.

Lines Composed in the Shadow of the Richmond Bridge

Shameful residue of impulse, unwritten
Letters of insult and adieu dissolved
Without trace by pure sightless passing time,
Thoughts nourished in naked sleepless night
Fracture into detachment. Surrender,
Rise. Smokeless dawn before refineries fire.
For once the city shines out clear to morning
For the earthly walker, whose overexposure
To the heavens makes a horizon sans
God seem also one without hope of pardon,
Playful in its backlash against freedom
As a scorpion to whom a man's tethered,
For the pets we keep reflect us—glassy
Eyed and garish, corpselike in the sportful dawn.

Lone Figure on Shattered Horizon

Could it be deconstruction's everything,
The whole of life a process of breaking down
In which one reaching for the shot brakes soon knows
All there is to learn about unhinged impulse,
But the big sudden blows that come or seem
To come from outside are the ones
That do the real work? While damage controls
Its minions, suppressing liberties with
A tyrant's power, shame keeps them from showing
The bruises all at once. Then there are the blows
That come from within. Reactor core of pain,
Language sits like a forgotten package
On the bench in a terminal somewhere
You passed through on your way to this end.

Vigil

In a nutshell life must be undergone oh
Eternity conscious moment: bounded
By ghostly faces of loved ones hovering
In muted antiseptic light, patient
Wishes to interpret slow ebbing of dear
Life as escape rather than mere extinction,
But exhaustion yields to conflicting
Testimonials. Abba, father. A vast
Sponge arrives to wash away all this drastic
Gloom like so much bad metaphysics:
The calm gesture of the doctor holding it,
His majestic voice, the acquiescence forced
From the survivors at the sad bedside
Who have only themselves left to save now.

Greed

In the forest it is cold. How can it be
Colder in the cities? It's as though we were
Practicing the art of filigree.
There's something eccentric, cranky, obtuse
About it, like a castaway's note in a
Bottle. Dialectical unfolding of
Slinky-toy history, life coils itself
Slowly, and then uncoils, descending the stairs
Negative reaction by negative
Reaction. We thought we were only here to please,
Yet as in that old painting of the peasants' feast
The banqueter represents the destroyer.
Eating is not only feeding oneself,
It is digging one's teeth into something.

Christmas on Telegraph

Shoppers rush past frozen images unseen,
In bright synthetics Sierra skiers ski
Through snowdead woods on blurred storewindow TV.
In the forest it is cold. How can it be
Colder in the cities? Street people crouched
Under Amoeba's protective arcade mouth
Such big round starving O's: oxygen balloons
Lifting off to perfect freedom, no strings—
A pity they can't float off in them.
Peace, brother. I can spare the buck or pass it.
Just breathing commits one to everything—
To life—which can't be purchased on this street
Where ravenous as sheer presence Christmas lights
Up human appetites for guilty pleasures.

Academic Tremor

Shaky domain from ivory watchtower surveyed:
Marking time's fagged essays, mean cigarette ends
Litter wet pavement where students stand
With books, wreathed in ethereal mists
Like wraiths or ghosts in pale chemises,
Smoking and talking beneath tall dark brown trees.
Through fog a grey girl's face looms hard as a board.
The fault lies quiet, yet the seismograph moves.
The grey girl's raised eyebrows thin as two new moons
Bespeak imagined dispossessions. Those eyes'
Tragedy ought to be grave. This is more like
Pathos, where silly ranges into strange
And dead objects secure power over life,
Muting the needle's stirrings along the rift.

January Storm

Sails of gulls flaring out in white above
The flooded landing track signal storms at sea—
Power lines blown down, and great redwood branches,
Waterlogged and groaning, thrown to the ground,
While swinging from its hinges, an unmoored gate
Cries out to cloud-black skies like a lost child.
Standing in the rain, interpreting these signs
To mean nature never meant us to be here:
Sentinels with eyes blind as Milton's, two tall
Stone dogs stand in the sideways rain and listen,
Wild wind noise like a banshee screaming "sister!"
To the neutered brother darkness out there
Which sounds back its nothing-engendering wail,
Night sifting the peace out of Pacific.

Wet Petals

Black cars throb past pavements blue with rain.
Soot black air under candlestick-like street lamp.
The pavement burns. A sentence forms. Black puddles
Gather leaf matter. Particles of dead mind,
Language massing without message: twisted
Ghosts pissing the grammar of the rain
Sift lights from skies black as an attic lost
Out of a child's head. Shutters pound in the wind
For years on end, nights on earth unending.
Something in your head flaps in the banging gusts
Self perplexed like the hang dog blond man
In the black rain in the Blue Dahlia
Who finds in the Lake the false face every
Hang dog seeker after truth is looking for.

Return of the Native

Rain shafts riddling me as I pace along
On sodden leaves and slush, with traffic splashing
Up a spume of dirty water on Henry.
A bald, brain-challenged cartoon boy strolls boldly
Out of a blurred past, becoming me,
Becoming enfeebled, leaning on a cane.
A beehive culture's no place for bonding
Systems of apes. Society will never work.
Miwoks ground acorns in holes in these rocks.
Wet night gives way to sodden, endarkened
Dawning. A new ancient day, already aged,
Encroaches: dead light, leaving liquid shades
To reign. Indigenes once trudged this spot
In sturdy muteness, crouched, stooping in the rain.

Forbearance

You bear a charmed life, but the air bites shrewdly.
The heart must bear the longest part. But of what—
That something for which you bear to live, just
Barely? Bareheaded in a hard condition,
The to-and-fro conflicting wind and rain
Bear down on you, and bear tolerance away.
You are a bearer of very little brain, and long
Words bother you. What can be brought to bear
Also must be borne. Bear with it, and your
Bearing will enlarge. Your words will bear you out.
Bring patience to bear, and bear in mind
The heavy bear that goes with you, weighing
You down. Bearing up under it's no use:
Asses are made to bear, and so are you.

Role Reversal

I can suck melancholy out of a song
By singing it, mourned the diffident artiste.
This rough and wintry weather lasts so long,
The rain it raineth every day.
Once, singing for my dinner, I was at best
Variously successful, yet pleased with
What I got. I loved the heat of the sun,
Ambition struck me as idiotic.
I got the idea of imitating the sun,
Smothering off my beauty from the world,
Letting iron clouds close in over me;
Then when I pleased I'd be myself again,
The more wanted the more wondered at,
Just by showing my face bring down the house.

Drama in Three Dimensions

A glimpse of plywood struts reminds you of
The guy's futility who tried to build
The diorama of the Globe Theatre,
For plays need living actors and a stage
And these distant, changed days come
So bare of scenic devices. The moon's down.
When the director requires dawn to break
The electricians will be summoned,
Special effects produce the liquid doors
Through which you'll step, leaving behind a childhood
Humble as the ripest mulberry, or turn
Aside to comment in a whisper that soars
Above the heads of a knowing audience,
Arrested spies behind a fourth wall.

Through This Long Winter of Freakshows and Floods

Our school a play, the play a carnival
In which the fool was me, the clown was me,
Mentor and tormentor in one role
Leaving you to wow the class, girl sawn in two,
Leaving me, that comic character, stranded
As the waters rose, me and that scrawny cat,
Half wild, on our raggedy raft in the flood,
An upside down bumbershoot afloat above
Air ducts, vents, chimneys, tv antennae—
And when the raindrops weirding down
From unindulgent heavens threatened
Finally to engulf us, that little cat
Jumped in a pan set out to catch leaks
And started rowing toward morning

To the Mistress of the Sailor's Rest

The antiquarian spirit sown in you
By your years among these splendid wrecks—
The venerable Capt. Gimp; his grizzled,
Toothless, brandy-breathing mate; the ship's
Surgeon, an addict with an erring knife;
The idiotic cabin boy, poking with
Idle digit every crevice below decks;
The blunt armorer, blazing at forges
Long consigned by history to scrap;
The daft sailmaker, whose billowy canvas
Illusions are to these leaden wharfside skies
What poems once were to real life,
And are about as much use to it now—
Will pave your days with doubtful sunken treasures.

Foolish Kingdom

If they had a king of fools I could wear that crown
And you would not die laughing because I'd wear it proudly.
You'd know where the door is and how to use it.
Outside there'd no doubt be another world,
Vassals of all sorts and kinds aimlessly
Milling at the fringes of this foolish kingdom,
Not yearning for the liberty that won't free them,
Hopping clouds of thought that revolve around you,
Craning their necks like starwatchers in Babylon,
Contributing their upward gaze in lieu
Of prayers in a language that escapes them
To your slow silences, your love of reading alone,
Your red hair, queenly detachment from authority,
The shade of Prussian blue you steep into life.

Adrift in Rue Street

While future tense exerts tendrils from below
A cold sun nods its dull head on its shoulder,
Doesn't want to rise. Prim girls at high service,
Anorexic seedlings clasp thin arms
To washed-out skies. Fearing day's depredations,
They won't open to a doubtful paradise
Of starved, rachitic-looking fennel stalks
Dotted with wild onions. Would you? To one
Adrift in Rue Street, spring's got no choice
But come back, iris and narcissus,
Chinese clouds, parades of teapot blues
Promising a moony indecision
Heralded by birds, who complete the picture
When spring comes, seeping down from upper worlds.

February Variations

Skin's still chilled but inside being warms
Rain stops as if to listen, plum tree rains down
Then in wind the frothy blossoms blow around
A random swirl, a foam of snowlike grains
Mothy white consolation flags unfurled
Victory banners tattered by a pelting blue
Flurry of quick flakes that overtakes you
You look, spring's unsaid promise hits
With a kissing lightness, a spray, faint show
Of force delicate as expectation
These are the flowers that bloom between storms
Drifting earthward, loose pieces of star
Plasm that slowed in transit between worlds
End up here for the sake of variation

March Morning

Wan dolls' false indigo, thrown against the cold,
Comes out water color, faded blue as souls
Laundered and fluttering on a breezy line,
Too late to freeze, too early to dry out
A sky drained of brilliance, stuffed with wet grey-white.
Awaited, spring refuses to be pushed.
Something in its latecoming promises a crush
Of sighs to follow like the mourning iris—
Its petals tissue-thin, folded on themselves,
A skin as delicate as mist or tears
Limp in morning drizzle, soft as daylong fog
That shrouds the dull head in cotton wool,
Stupidly drooping. Then arrives the rose,
A thorn of beauty to crown all this dumbness.

Cortege of Irises

Bowing and stooping as sad actors do
When slate skies close, they face an unexcited
Audience that finds their colors faint as gauze:
Mourning iris, furling cerulean flags
Of handmade paper soft and limp as muslin,
Pearls, doves, weeping violets, pouting blues,
Also a rust brown hybrid, stippled, tall
With saffron private parts drooping in the rain,
Take cold rewards from clouds that loom like judges,
Fold pale chilled arms back in on themselves,
Shrink out of the way of new blooms to come,
Whether their bending provokes weak wet applause
Or shows a blank disdain that quiets it,
As the curtain falls on their too brief run.

Old Album

No past bears presents to equal being there.
Put that book away. Ghost faces, doubtful gifts:
Word apparitions washed ashore to perish
As life roars by in blue reverie blurs,
Tulips incandescent as the rain that beats them
When March storms unleash this wild dance of forms.
Presence comes before being, being before
There was ever a you or me. Ancient
Grief will go from you as from sorrowing songs
Sorrow goes, leaving nothing for you
To whom everything belongs because your poor
Defenseless inner self has gaily sailed
Into the room like all the modern languages
Coming down to us, so you could say these things.

Resolution

When I went out at dawn I found a small grey
Bird hardly larger than my little finger,
Dead yet still warm, breast feathers nestled in
By a bright green caterpillar, fallen
From dark overhanging branches above,
Harbinger of what? In this cold spring of storms,
Finding brief rest in a death boat fashioned
From two large umbrella shaped ivy
Leaves set afloat upon an oily puddle
To swirl that tiny watch-pocket flier
Away toward worlds it never heard of,
Life settles by gravity into future's mud
Where despite everything else that happens
All losses are restored, and sorrows end.

On the Beach

The storm has ended and death steps back
Into the waters once more. All our troubles
Are behind us once and for all.
The moon looks down in single glory.
The apocalyptic view of the world
Supposes things do not repeat themselves.
But they do. And they do. And they do.
The sky clouds up. A new storm comes on.
Apocalyptic thinking presumes
All this has never happened before
And will never happen again. I know,
As the moon beams down on the photo-plankton,
All this will never happen again, too.
Wisdom is cold and to that extent stupid.

The Black Weir

To woo the heathen priests he healed with a leaf
Of shamrock, symbol of the three-headed god.
Under his heel, the serpent powers objected,
Were tricked into the black weir anyway.
He chased out the weird supernatural
Residuum, some crusty old creatures
Who hung around cave mouths, smoking, tippling.
Still my wearing of the green to the Chinese
Jawbreaker proved less than lucky. Pity.
You can't build clouds. Futures you shape in dreams self
Erase. You came in here for mercy and grace
After your measure, found darkness, confusion,
Mystery, blank space. St. Paddy's Day,
You lose your last teeth: an Irish commonplace.

Deli Pastry Counter

Still I want to live and enjoy living
Through my brain, that illuminated screen
On which phantoms of my thoughts are shown. True or
False, brief presence, flashed on a neutral pane,
Withdraws rapidly into a dumb half-life,
A door locked against a perfect world,
The shrinking breathmark where I pressed my nose
A moment ago. Now I'm not that person.
Others go ahead, I stay in one place,
And on these occasions, like raisins in a cake,
What gives my thoughts their lustre is a light
Shining on them from behind the glass display.
They do not themselves glow, nor does the window,
Hunger having left just this faint moist trace.

Video Store Window Display

Like so many tiny pixie tv's
Flashing messages to each other all night
The hundred billion neurons in your brain
Replace identity as such with deep
Cosmic gossip while your body's arrested
In mid flight back toward an old savannah—
A hundred billion neurons seeking shelter,
Losing that deep self because you're asleep,
Lost in your dreams, a functional state
Of your brain lapsing into disappearance,
Your brain not bothering to compute you,
Your sense of who you are going up in smoke,
Though if the soul be several not one
There's only now and that now has its presence.

These Truths We Hold Self-Evident

If with outer eye you see just what's shown,
Inner's lit by a glow of special pleading:
Wishful thinking dressed up as knowledge
Commits you to the unknown, as though secrets
Propped a hedge against the hurtful tide
Truths of human practice motivate at you.
Still precious privacy, grooming for the dive
It fears to take back into that harsh fact swirl,
Lets you pluck up courage in your heart of hearts,
That bivalve mollusc like a cockleshell,
Hollow muscular organ which by pumping
Keeps up the circulation of the blood.
In love it's split and piteous, but no harm done
Diastolically's completely one-sided.

Trust

Holding the world in the hollow of one's
Hand, that role formerly accorded gods,
Yet keeping that hand open as a heart,
The magician king knows the shipwreck
Will happen, hears seas crashing, hysterical
Screams, final splitting of beams, feels victims' tears—
The whole spectacle recapitulated
By Miranda, who's seen it from farther off
Than we, stationed in the conditional mood—
Yet too knows all now not only must be
But will be well, in fact perhaps always was,
For the eyewitness' transfixed iteration
Seemed even at the time to be missing
Something essential, some element of trust.

Prospero's Prosperity

In the end, the constellations emerge
Rich and bewildering in paratactic
Defiance of the night's strange high blankness—
But don't changes always illuminate that way,
A logic of radiance, no signs or sighs,
Only stony silences crossing lines with
The phone in eternity that rings and rings,
The demimondaine who throws cold arms
Around the Platonist under these dry stars
To give old myths new issue, this island's
Implicit privilege dissolving
The deeper into these seas one's book sinks,
Leaving attention fixed on not the power
Of the magician king, but the victims' tears?

The Sorcerer

It is a brilliant use of old device,
The masquerader masquerading as what
She in fact is, while the rest of us
Remain ignorant of just who we are.
Funny, the child's chatter gathers giant
Resonance from echoing beneath awareness'
Overarching dome; this planetarium
In which darkness softly explodes fills up
With showers of sparks we alone perceive,
Music, song, dance, clowning, roguishness,
Life's blackest moments seeming uncontrolled,
Worlds whirling toward immediate ruin
So that in the long run good may prevail—
I have made such provision in my craft.

Equivocal Salute

Hail the Time Goddess, before whom we bow down
These sad arms we were not meant to carry
Into wars of the heart for reasons
More serious or less pressing than desire's;
Who demands of us only falling apart
Cell by cell, a tax of her possessiveness;
Into whose fealty each of us is borne
From limits far remote, where other rules hold,
As into the unbending spell of a lover
Whose gain is identical with your own loss,
On wings that seem to fail as if waterlogged
Or clogged with ice too thick to thaw—patina
Of her impossible distance, tolerant
Of no temporal extension save her own.

TORN FROM AN OLD ALBUM

The Cycle

In the womb, selfless harmony,
undifferentiated light,
a rich drifting in dreams from which
before the strange generations
chance to state their wailing cases

one tumbles down into real
life such awful distance. Splat. Two
persons now seem distinct, mother
and one, pending apparition
of others, who, farther, fainter,

grow at last remote. Then years and
years of solitude proceeding
straight toward a hole in the ground
occupied by just one. The end.
Then the above over again.

Name Day

> "I have no name,
> I am but two days old."
> What shall I call thee?
>
> "I happy am,
> Joy is my name."
> Sweet joy befall thee!
> —Blake

The happy infant in the bassinet
has a smile large and round, there being no

more teeth in his mouth than are in yours now,
though it's evident that crying out loud

in wonder is something he probably
is here before you doing one more time

than you will ever again attempt it,
peering in cracked mirror of past for clue

a blackened shadow in the photograph
conceals forever—the name, that birth mark

as indelible as color of eyes,
of skin—a doubtful given taken back

in the end along with all else human,
whatever differentiated you.

Catholic School Courtyard, Chicago

I

Child of a lesser god
hair slicked down with care,
altar boy surplice too
long over black cassock
under which stick out shiny
little wingtip shoes
squints out at you, oh
ominous shadow casting
snapshot taker in
asphalt yard of St.
Catherine's School,
Austin Boulevard,
Holy Thursday nineteen
forty eight. The great
weight of time increases
its burden with the years,
the furrowing of the
youthful brow, peering in
to a future neither
so strong nor so bright
as the sun, is proved
prophetic by the ancient
passage rite through
which withdrawal of the
shadow of the father
merely overshadows
the confusion of the sun,
relieving no one. So

soon gone, so solely
alone, in the fluid
and banal continuum.

II

And only then, only after
the sense of loss locks in,
when reasons uttered
by self to self to
condone or evade pain
are at last exhausted,
does the obvious fact
register, that this
shining day of seasons
changing, of bright wind,
and sun, forty five
years ago and counting—
with time's glaring brick
backdrop, dark gothic
school windows closed in
to contain whatever grim
or dim or maybe simply
empty truths experience
holds, its sad pathos,
its distance, its last
chance sense of things that
though without them one
can never be anything
but separate, still
one can't any longer
even want to grasp—was
in fact occasion

of its clearly unjoyous
subject's first earnest,
inglorious, reluctant,
holy communion.

My Father on the Riverside & Great Northern (Little Railway, Dells, Wisconsin)

Here he is riding a miniature train
and here I am, in our back yard, engaged

with my train to nowhere. Locomotive and
tender, in close-up, appear bound for

somewhere new, when seen from ground view, but a
long shot reveals the track begins and ends

in our back yard. The blanket over the
sandbox protects the sand. History

is not so forgiving as the human, sad,
common memory of time, which makes of

all effort perhaps no special shrine but
at least tries at last to understand it.

Buddy

There is an obscure man named Willard Clark,
a hapless itinerant sign painter,

ad designer, thwarted sometime artist;
who marries Irene Loretta Cann in

Chicago around turn of the century,
and just after First War, in which he takes

reluctant part, in letters home betraying
perhaps something of canker to come, dies,

leaving behind two sons. The older walks
into Lake Michigan one day, and not

back out. The younger, last in the male line,
walks in from normal world one day, finds Irene

on her way out of that world on kitchen
floor. He runs for help: she's gone before it

arrives. He becomes, though clearly gifted,
the unhappiest of men, a drinker,

violent, and self-destructive. My dad.
His big sisters, who idolized him, called

him "Bud," "Buddy": little brother. I have
before me a photo of him making

a silk screen. He's wearing a clean white shirt,
dark tie, blue serge dress trousers: must be

looking for work. Wavy hair slicked in place ("He
was quite the collar ad," someone later

said), but his face though still youthful's begun
already to show signs of that inverted

pain and rage, bloated mask of the bad
genius of the rest of his life—all those

humiliating, dreary jobs, salesman
of decalcomania, of cardboard

boxes, looks, wits slowly decomposing,
Friday nights my mother out in the car

combing West Madison Street bars, faint hope
of finding him before somebody else

lays hands on his paycheck. They couldn't, I
suppose, understand, not just each other,

but what it was had so gone wrong for
him—why, though he wanted, and worked at, living—

worked at it—*wanted* life—as all of us do—
he just couldn't stand it.

The Chief

for my grandfather, Thomas Patrick Kearin

Gentle, strapping Irish youth, on loose in rambling world,
He came down to Chicago from Dakota,
Lit street lamps with long poles in gaslight days,
Piloted a streetcar, then went on the Force,
Walked beat, was at Valentine's Day Massacre,
Though happily for him several hours late.

Never a violent man for all his size.
Years later, town paper memorialized
His donating stolen bikes to poor kids,
Awarding speeding ticket to Barney
Oldfield. My birthday by contingency of fate
Falling on same day as his, I got his name.

West Side cop cronies called him Chief, wife and
Doting daughters Daddy. Drove us coast to coast
In big blue and white riverboat De Soto;
Wore a big pearl Stetson; toted in his great
Coat a leather holstered Colt revolver
Put high up safe when he came in the house.

In old snapshot he supervises destruction
Of bootleg liquor in civic thoroughfare.
Though vigorous axes wielded to fell
All that potential gaiety must have
Inflicted a chill within his own heart
As well, you wouldn't guess it from his pose.

A head above his fellows in plainclothes
And a straw boater, he dominates
The photo-op, his own probable regret
For precious spirits so gratuitously spilled
Well concealed beneath bluff public cop
Demeanor, mourning wasted pleasures.

In another, he heads a march down Lake Street,
Tall, hale, proud, nightstick swinging to beat of drum.
Kids ride bikes with spokes tricked out in bunting.
Is one of those handlebar-lolling kids me,
Marooned in a lost America neither
Nostalgia nor irony encompasses?

When he came to die, I was long gone
Over a wide continent and a cold ocean
(Sad note from mother was my only notice).
Strange though that years later his mute faith I'd one
Day redeem not just his investment of
Trust but his name somehow still haunts.

Torn from Old Album

Pale intent wondering little
man with serious fedora
casts short shadow in flat wide
light of his grandfather's front yard
squinting dutifully into
a doubtful future's narrowing
eye. Years of rain and snow and sun
rush by, a blinding prospect. Night
falls and everybody dies
back into the faded album
pages, white blurs effacing youth's high

gloss. Loss, not yet more than a word
for what you simply can't find—toy,
book, sock—lurks unprepossessing
as among shades huddled ahead,
consciousness emerges: time stuns
it with one blow, stands it back up
so as to knock it down over
again. Still, life continues to
play hopefully into the hand
behind the lens, fighting against
blinking; and then the shutter clicks.

Forties Scene

Here he's about seven: big serious forehead,
little fedora, little man, he holds,

or seems to drag, his baby brother, whose
eyes are closed. Bare winter trees project long

stark shadows. The days are short, light thin and
for those smiling family ghosts lined up in

invisible ranks behind the peony
bushes—this time of year no more than scrub

grey stubs of dumb roots hidden underground—
no providential dividend for brave

investment of years promised remains, save
this fading, hollow sound—life's dim echo?

Urban Pastoral Scene (mid-1940s)

In time we find three children, two charming girls,
one boy, enjoying picnic amid junk
strewn vacant lot in life's brief eclogue of
passage through ambient wild creation.
The kid in the middle's me, sucking on
some milk, while the two girls—script verso
identifies them as Jane and Suellen,
cherubic if imperfectly
recalled twin pigtailed-blond secret
sharers of archaic lunch time—munch huge
sandwiches that dwarf the tiny fists with
which they hungrily clutch them, much as life's clutched,
as though a whole world were there to be eaten.

Fall of the Hero

Encroaching twilight shadows on
brick tenement wall against
which fat boy in archaic dome
peaked football helmet, shoulder pads,

high-hipped padded pants stands
squinting into low western sun
(late October or November,
1948) appear to

creep up wood stairs he stands on in
such a way as to threaten him
with falling into some deeper
understanding—life's knock on door?

Sad Goddess

First Marilyn Monroe memory
involves being in back seat of car
driven by youthful friend's father, who
tells joke that hinges on assertion
that even if Marilyn Monroe

were bald, etc. We are on Congress Street
driving west around Wabash, I think,
since we are passing Minsky's Burlesque.
The entire past, viewed in black and white,
inspires sensation of having dirt

under collar, sleazy dim subtext,
secret embarrassment, not knowing,
never ceasing to wonder about,
and being continually surprised
how anything in nature functions.

Collegiate (1959)

Crewcut jug eared foolish
in crisp collegiate sport
shirt buttoned down à la
the Kingston Trio, he's

Mr. Big Man on Campus,
has a girl on each arm,
stands in the center
of an immaculate

world. His smile with teeth
invites that world to join
his party. Behind him,
the wall of the school

corridor encloses a
fire hose in glass casing,
silent emblem of the
hygiene that protects

this scene from the future.

Old Photo

What life means: photo of
(barefoot? can't see) crewcut
boy on pier, nineteen fifties—what
does he know of what's ahead?
Behind, a lake. What bubbles up
out of life's strange effervescence
but the endless past, with its stupid
foam and buoyancy? Who *would*
plunge back in and live it all
over again, just to wipe hope's
youthful wonder off its face?

Dog Jumping to Stand Rock

The leap of faith is planless to witness. It
is as much an accident as elation
always is. Still why is it that without the
energy of youth to serve as an updraft
one cannot catch the wind so readily as

one did at Dells, Wisconsin, July '60?
The dog caught in mid air leaping between two
rock formations is a moment of time that's
elsewise lost in the swift race from gate to gate.
The young man who captured it in his camera

is long gone, though I still bear his fate in its
full dark illumination out there like a
miner's light that throws the past into shadow
continually: in front of me mercy
unknowing, behind me the weight of a name.

The Irish

A people generous, hospitable, gay
In the old sense, lovers of music of harp,
Dancers and storytellers, given to singing
And gaming, to venial social crimes,
A prevalent flowing of whiskey, and
Civic creed of *ubi est mea* (where's mine?).

My grandmother Kathleen Gaynor, a lovely
Tiny woman born beneath a thatched roof
In County Westmeath, sent me off to England
With a tear, last time I ever saw her;
That it wasn't so much my going pained her
As *to where* took me years to comprehend.

Not till I got to Cambridge did I learn
That Cromwell's deciding his decimations
Of Wexford and Drogheda were not the work
Of man, but a righteous judgment of God
To prevent the effusion of future blood,
Proved Providence held no place for her people.

The Irish (Later)

Prematurely ageing was the most sanguine
Way I could think to describe to myself
The wrinkled, pockmarked, twisted, misgiving
Old geezer-visage whose quick scared eyes caught mine
In the mirror at the cancer surgeon's office.

Then again, perhaps maturity remains
A forever unattainable goal to
A member of that most childish or was
It childlike people in the universe (as
The Sinnead O'Connor song has it), the Irish.

Later, office phoned: I forgot to sign check.
Through a child's eyes the old always seemed
Astonishingly simpleminded in
What I now myself experience, old—
A perfect simulacrum of their dotage.

JOE

(*In memoriam* Joe Brainard, 1942-1994)

Joe

Nineteen sixty
seven, spring, the
climactic stop
on Ted's Cook's Tour
of Lower East
Side: Joe's tiny
flat at Third and
B, stacked wall to
wall with works in
progress amassed
for his "big break
through" flower show
at Fischbach, which
would make *Art News*
cover. Nervous,
polite, Joe took
interruption
like a perfect
gentleman: still
you guessed you were
interrupting:
and of course you
were. He offered
us Pepsis, small
talk; he smoked; then
we left, and he
painted.

*

Five months later
up in Vermont,
while the rest of
us laid back in
or were swamped by
the thoughtless green
damp far northern
August days, Joe
paced, smoked, drank six
packs of Pepsi and
painted a trail
right through them, as
if weirdly wired
into a cool
steady drive to
make images.
When he snuck a
break for two hours
and we went to
Montpelier he
studied roadside
views so intently
I was sure works
were being sketched
out in his head
en route as Ron
drove. The day it
came time to go
back to New York
Joe walked off his
no-work nerves by
stalking around
outside the house.

*

Neither modest
nor shy will quite
encompass it,
more like knowing
everything
without having
to pretend it's
more than it is,
or less, or say
anything at
all about it,
either way. Like
his works, Joe had
this aura.

*

Didn't
he once say he
made a point of
believing in
all the major
religions, since
whether or not
"true," either way
each held its at
least possible,
conceivable
consolations?

*

It's May, moonlight
is probably
coming through those
pines outside the
upstairs window
at Kenward's house
where a tall and
skinny ghost with
horn rim glasses,
silent, thoughtful,
pacing, smoking,
is making works
without stopping.

Reflections

Vita

Like a pinball game played in reverse
Perhaps behind this whole story lies
An unhappy childhood conception
Of the Einsteinian universe. Routine measuring-rods
Of importance, such as the fact of other people's
Existence, no longer seemed to hold good
Without the usual bells and bumper pads as warning,
One's childish aspirations and fears exploded
Inward like tropical blossoms growing in slow motion
At the bottom of the ocean. Waving in ooze
The dimensions of things became irrevocably
Skewed, or was that just one's private vision,
One's inability to fathom the whole
Significance of human life? For instance the word
Silhouette, its meaning eroded as a stone
Under ten centuries of dripping by being repeated
Over and over through a three-week siege
Of rheumatic fever. One desperately imaged
Oneself to oneself as the only possible friend
In a world incapable of that communion. Now
And then glooms thickened, yet the little star of self-love,
Whose twinkle would encourage one through even
Deeper glooms to come, shone with a trustable
Brilliance like religion continually promised
Yet never seemed to deliver. What else?
Out of a goose-white moon hung over
The city night with a workmanship one
Oddly attributed to Longines the watchmaker's
Angels, who were trapped in a fold-a-bed by
Radio waves, distorted as they came, there grew a voice

Of something like adulthood, issuing from depths
Unspoken, as if some miniature shred of bone
Bounced on the mirror of a sleeping mind
Fell first in love with its own image, then sound
Asleep. Then, when one was not quite twelve,
The quest for reunion with a girl who had moved away,
The problem of the nature of time, the value
And significance of suffering and joy, alarums
Reverberating in dreams, and welling up from austere
Silence, converged in the muted threnody of the Dying
Trumpeter Boy, whose bright clear notes told all
Love was victorious, yet gravely flawed.
Like trumpet and echo, these reflections of a lonesome
    mind
Pretended the dream is a law to itself, while the child who
Forgets a quarrel with a rainbow grew into the one
Who writes this. Going anywhere? Stick around for a drink
If you've got time. You're bound to find parts and fractions
Of some kind of eternal creation
Going on, but the problem is always wanting
Something more. Oh, the radiations
Of energy to the circumference continue
To keep the houselights burning, but feeling gets short
Changed on days like this, like limbs still jerking
After removal of the head—a lively nervous reflex
Can hardly make up for one's failure over
A period of several years ever once to crack open
A can of smiles, and offer you one. After telling
You one's life, how can one depart without leaving the
    token
Amulet of a business card, at least. No further queries
    please.
The last box here is for filling in one's current address.

In this earthquake neighborhood, after last night's sharp
 crack
When one drifts off to sleep tonight it will have to be
Like allowing oneself to fall into something
Deep, like one's loved ones' despair for one,
Always so much less consoling than one's own.

Superannuated Boy

Perhaps in consequence of calamities that struck him early on
In his earnest progress toward a seemingly unattainable adulthood
The stamp of melancholia branded his most trifling bagatelles
Like a black flaw in a mood ring. The first person was his

Favorite figure of speech. The impressions of infancy having burnt
Into him like tattoos, he resented the impertinence of manhood.
Whatever was urgent and disturbing he studiously avoided
In favor of the small, reassuring rituals of everyday life.

In company he would commonly be suspected an odd
Fellow until he stammered out some senseless pun, which proceeded
To spill his character across the room like a bottle of ink
On a clean white tablecloth. Discretion appeared to elude him.

Though his conceptions rose, like someone standing up so as to be
Distinguished from everyone else in the room, above his utterances,
His cleverest impromptu remarks always showed flashes of the sweat
Of effort on their backs, as if he were merely trying to be witty.

In fact he struggled just to speak. He had a horror of being
Seen in public, and, as if it were a stranger, kept a wary
Eye upon the advances of age that should have entitled
Him to the general respect he affected to disdain. He did

Not conform readily to the march of time, but was dragged
Along in the procession. His manners lagged behind his
    years.
He was too much the boy-man. The *toga virilis* never sat
Gracefully on his shoulders. Indoors he always wore some
    kind of hat.

As We Grow Old

Like yen advancing in value against the dollar
Our sense of time grows more acute in proportion
To our inability to do anything with it
That's of use to anyone, or was it always this
Way? We have inklings of eternal sameness sometimes,
Then feel betrayed when depreciation sinks its gray fang.
Few things stay the same, so why shouldn't there be change
In us too? What malign agency drains from our brains
All the oils and juices that keep the flower growing?
What flower? Now we're even starting to forget things.
Still when we step back and try to gain some distance
From our own minds, we get this sense we're being followed
By yesterday's papers, which keep landing at our door
—O tempora O mores!—with a soft lamenting thud.

On the Growth of a Thin Skin

Don't be so quick to forgive and forget.
Whole empires have been built up out of perceived
Slights, all the more imposing for their special kind of dwarf
Grandeur. Anyone can be bolstered by flattery,
Whereas it takes an expert to conflate hints
Of genius from alleged insult. What else swells up
The creative self half so well as being convinced
One's the victim of a cold injustice? Exploded
Into the dimensions of a giant gas bubble
Composed of conceit, weighed down by vast
Gravity, and spinning at unimaginable speeds
Around a central negative core of deep
Dissatisfaction, one's vanity and pride
Attain the density of cosmic dark matter
For days at a time. Everyone would love
Discontent if they understood its mysteries.
Moreover, like most learned behavior
Sullenness is not closed off to any sincere prospective
Initiate. The first grievous sting of suspicion—
Say, after being cut on the street by a presumed friend—
Wears off after a few hours or days,
At which point you may begin to extract
From the wound that balm and honey of injured self
Righteousness which as everyone knows
Is Power. Forget true facts and sane
Inferences. An adept in the science of
Suspiciousness finds the galls themselves
Soothing, the trash of his reputation his obscurely desired
Briar patch. Have patience, and accept
Each erosion of your self-regard before

The hard weathers of the bad atmosphere
You invent to surround yourself with
As a gift horse. Go home, make the worst of it.
Lock the door, turn off the phone and reject
Any insinuation you may have misinterpreted things.
Somewhere there is joy, and you are left out of it,
You hope. Your best pal called you touchy behind
Your back, and the news of it's just reached
You. Nothing's as delicious as the ink
Of a poison pen. You'll have a black tongue for weeks
As you reflect darkly on earlier disaffections
From the same source, real or deduced
By the illogical hounds of a deranged
Sleuth. Study how not to take a joke.
Image yourself to yourself as the sole
Possible friend in a world incapable of that
Exalted communion. The gloom thickens, but
The little star of self-love will twinkle to
Encourage you through deeper glooms than these.
Never forget the very essence of what's right
Has been drained out of the depleted planet
Entirely, except for those precious traces
Secreted by and nurtured in your own
Solitary heart. Expanding to populate
At least one rich hemisphere with yourself,
You leave the Arabia Deserta
Of the earth's other half to the aforesaid
Insulters, fated forever to remain
Strangers to your curious private delight
In their oversight: failing to acknowledge
Your preeminence is their problem not yours. You're secure
In your cultivated hypersensitivity.
How shall one say it? To forego the idea

Of having been ill-used represents the ultimate sacrifice,
At which the sole votive celebrant
Would be yourself. Wronged, you grow larger every moment
As the race shrinks, other persons gradually
Dwindling to sub-human while you're deified
In your own mind by stages. And now you reach the acme:
That rainy, sulky afternoon in your room
On which you first find yourself able to presume
To judge the world. Self-exclusion's pure bliss
From this privileged vantage: the point at which
Sense of benefit forgot merges into meditation
Of general injustice, and accidental omission,
Far from all possibility of forgiveness,
Takes on the value which a requiting of love might
Hold for longing paramours: the whole flattering
Superstructure thrown up by pride upon
A foundation of deliberate misunderstanding
Has become the palace of your hurt feelings,
Out of which, permanently joyously
Sulking, you need never again set foot.

The Suspect

I don't have a single complete suit of clothes
In my intellectual closet. Unsystematic,
I beat up a little game, and leave it to
Knottier and more robust heads to track it down.

The light that lights me is not steady
And polar, but shifty, like the flickering
Beams of the police flashers brightly hitting
My mutilated wax bust of John Wayne.

The germs of my best thoughts hatch *ab ovo*.
Under questioning, I'll throw out a word or two
Merely to be suggesting something,
Just don't ask me to say anything under oath.

To mature a proposition till it's ripe
Is beyond me. I bring my corn to market still
In the green ear. No wonder I'm under house
Arrest, awaiting further developments as they arise.

Classic Clown

Only light in the house beams on me, showing
Pindrop poise before the wall of noise moment;
There's quite a din when I fall on my sword.
Didn't someone say words are swords? Dying
Day brings sounds of angels sighing high up
In dark tiers of a numinous sky. Fresh clown
Tears fly. Last thing I see is my life flashing
Before my eyes. Last things I hear are the vast

Basso of the cannon going off, my swift
Whistling emergence out of the barrel,
The lion tamer's laugh, my strange ballistics
As I soar over the highwire walker's pole
And out through the hole in the tent peak.
Heaven bent on my grim mission I create
A diversion that lasts till intermission,
Then get on my comic tricycle and ride.

A monkey face punched through a paper
Hoop, how do you like my painted smile?
There's quite a din when I plunge on my sword.
Didn't someone say words are rubber swords? Day
Dying brings sounds of angels sighing high up
In dark tiers of a numinous sky's fake clouds:
Clown wheezing, pedals furiously pumping,
Me trying to climb a loop up into that sky.

Faint Heart

When the night's wavelike sound mosaic breaks up into its
    nonidentical pieces
With the wind wailing out of the Gothic theme forest like this
Scary as a diva with a screaming migraine,
Whistling in the vast dark as a sign of valor's
Vastly overrated. The monsters aren't at all impressed
Or for that matter anything more than mildly amused
The way a cat tosses and catches a terrified mouse
    appetizer
By your show of bravery. They see a nerveless hectoring
Little fellow exposed in all his aching selfhood, and find it
    wonderful
To divert a share of their own animal spirits to him
Just to even up the score a little. You can't blame them
For your fear. In fact you haven't got the strength
To furnish so much as a tolerable bluster,
And huffing isn't the same thing as courage.

Tergiversation

Who are you? If you remembered, the act of turning your
    back
Might not seem so attractive. But you don't know: who are
    you
To talk? It's strange how, tossing and turning
In your solitary sleepless meditations, the more you lord
It over the sheets, thrashing, shifting, tumbling,
The deeper you sink. More frequently than a politician
You change sides. You lie now stretched out, now at an
    oblique
Angle, or transverse, head and feet forming a great
Cross. It's strange how big you seem to yourself,
In your petty king-like sway over your helpless, longsuffering
Pillow. Within these four corners you are absolute
Monarch of space. But the giant of self-importance wastes
Away once the sleepy embassy from Nature comes.

Against Early Rising

You only dream any dream once. We choose to linger
Abed awhile to digest, snatching from
Forgetfulness the wandering images which darkness
Projected in a confused masque. Dream police
Show up toting poles and nets to drag into daylight
The struggling and half-vanishing nightmare
And haul it still protesting aboard the boat:
Work necessary as food in keeping body and soul
From each other's throats. We have too much respect
For these spiritual communications to let them go
Unfished-up. We are not so careless
As that Imperial Forgetter of his dreams—
Once we dreamed Sid Caesar played him—who
Needed a seer to remind him of the form
Meaning assumes, when it materializes out of
Night visions. They signify more than waking
Things, we're tempted to think more and more as more
Nearly we approach by years to the shadowy
World whither we are always hastening,
Rehashing our dreams. Morning passes
Over us vaguely, like a coating of wax.
Our biological clock appears to have struck
A submerged rock and sunk with all hands
Pointing to midnight. We feel superannuated.
We contract alliances with ghosts. The media
Of dreams seem to be abstracted, like tigers
Who know we are about to be thrown to them
But have no taste for us. Therefore we choose to
Dally with our visions. The sun has no purpose
Of ours to light us on our way to, so why get up?

Artificial Light

Without it, what savage unsocial nights
Our ancestors must have spent! All those deadly
Winter nocturnes in caves and unillumined icy
Fastnesses: they must have lain around and
Grumbled at one another in the dark like the blind,
Fumbling each other's features for the wrinkle of a smile.
What tedious repartee must have passed! Perhaps
This accounts for the dullness of much archaic
Poetry, whose somber cast is notorious and must
Have derived from the traditions of those
Long unlanterned nights. Jokes came in with candles.
How did they see to pick up a pin, if they
Had any? How did they get dinner down? Think of
The mélange of chance carving that must have
Ensanguined dining after dusk! Lights out,
Not even love's what it's cracked up to be.
The senses absolutely give and take
Reciprocally. One wants to know whether that's
An elbow, a knee, or the night table
Before one returns the favor of a friendly nudge.
Wasn't it by the midnight taper all writers once digested
Their meditations? By that same light we ought
To approach them, if we ever expect to catch
The tiger-moth of inspiration that dances
In the word *incandescent*.

The Allée d'Argenson

The making of *Casablanca* was pure accident.
These two persons didn't have to meet
One rainy day, watching chess players at
The Café des Étoiles. She spoke first.
"I am your jester, or possibly you are mine."
Two kinds of people are reading this poem.
All life's a mosaic of what-ifs. Rick's
Customers were played by real refugees.
Studio wanted Michèle Morgan in the role of
Ilsa, the woman with divided loyalties.
Practical joker twins wrote the dialogue.
Every afternoon at five, Diderot
Went for a stroll in the Palais-Royal.
He was seen alone there meditating
By a giddy-looking young girl, or
Was it Diderot himself who looked giddy.
Who would believe anything endearing
Could result from such a life, let alone
Enduring. Yet people stop here to this day.

Comic Interpretation

This isn't one of those old funnybooks
Where Popeye & Co. keep on coming back
To live their lives exactly the same way
Over and over again, sans apparent
Reasoning behind the idiotic
Reiteration of the rhyme, which,
Like life itself, tender plasmic issue,
Concession to nature's force majeure,
Comes squashed between juicy, doughy buns
Constantly headed into that gaping
Maw sunken into the kisser of Wimpy,
Is it? Flung to earth beneath ancient treehouse,
Tattered, yellowed, weather-rotted, comic,
The text of an inauthentic destiny
Yields up its cargo of hidden clues
Like a reluctant oracle, its faint flame
Of vision by this time so obscured
As to permit every mis-application:
E.g. when Sweepea, like a Blakean worm
Crawls from Olive Oyle's warm cartoon arms
Into a millennial tape-loop
Safe from the abuse potential of
A vile Bluto bearing down—what else is new—
Do we proclaim the perfect p.c. child?
Was Popeye a pipesmoker to prove his maleness?
Notwithstanding all that bulking-up
Produced by swinging from the rigging
Like a vegetarian monkey
Without a foundation in brute history
A bent frame bereft of moral spinach
Shouldn't have shipped out in the first place.

The Case of Miss Twitch

The breeze that filters through the palm fronds may be mild
As my private thoughts, advancing microscopically
Across the soft forest lawn chest hair wilderness
And then abruptly dropping off into your navel
Like when Little Lulu tumbles insouciantly into a manhole—
Am I in over my head? Loan me your cellular
Consciousness of the primal soup we swim in,
Starfish positioning ourselves deliciously to slide
Beneath the outriggers of the theme pier. From the terrace
I can hear the waves down on the beach slapping and
      pushing
At the sand, a small child with shovel and pail crying
To its mother, who lies there like overbroiled seafood
      beside it,
The buzz of a light plane skimming the water surface out a
      little
Farther than the farthest swimmers, the sound of a phone
      being dialled.

Astrolabe

Anxiety meter off. Here you are, lovely, sitting on the bed,
    and here I am, painting
In my head. We're watching Neil Young, anachronistic as a
    buffalo
In a lumberjack shirt, dolefully encase his songs in amber.
Out back I can hear the old time machine stretching its
    wings and warming
Up. They say Apollo was as old as the sun, yet always
    looked young,
Fingers flying over the strings, light streaming from his
    flowing locks,
Ignition sparks flaming out of the engine cowls you see
    when you look out
The carriage windows of time's winged chariot, racing
    toward the sun,
Reaching it, passing it, then racing and reaching for the
    moon,
Swinging back around, slingshotting out into the starry
    universe like a bus
With no brakes or headlights on a Mexican mountain road at
Midnight. It's getting late and the moon is climbing. Older,
    I'd still like to shine
My celebration in your eye. Because I'm still an idiot, with
    my
Shirt hanging out and hair down to my harmonica holder.

Heraldic Emblem

The Movies as Natural History

What freezes us into the frame like this,
Petrifying objects wherein life's congealed
Secrets lie like Sleeping Beauty waiting
To be awakened by the present's kiss:

The blood camellia that blooms in the syringe
To dissolve with pure smack in a white cloud
Which as his thumb presses down on the plunger
Roars like a train wreck into Vincent's arm;

The still-life aura—*nature morte*—that lights up
The compact, numinous Czech M-61
Submachine gun with huge silencer Butch spies
On the kitchen counter just as, setting down

The milk carton, he drops two Pop Tarts in
The toaster; the rabbit-trapped-in-carrot-patch
Expression frozen on Vincent's vacant face,
Surprise melting in sudden understanding,

As, tightening his belt after nature's call,
Toting *Modesty Blaise*, he enters
The kitchen and sees Butch; the question mark that
For one long moment hangs in both their and our eyes.

Living in a Simulation

It takes a thick skin to survive this
State of soft shock. They say we'll be
Living in a simulation tomorrow:
Like steam locomotive colliding with bullet

Train inside jello mold size of Toledo
Emotional commotion and noise won't so
Much as nudge the needle on the scale,
Flower world will open into space—first thought

Of this morning, vanishing tonight,
Limited yet total, all there is, precise
Catchall for soft shocks that never end
Yet hurt not, like grenades of playdough.

A Wanderer in the World

The dawns, awesome runaway fire engine affairs—
And the winter nights out here, stupid, unyielding
Beasts to grapple. Thin air, streaming clouds: high plateau
Country, inhabited by a people simple
From years of isolation and inbreeding: they think
It's their job to take care of the world, which they run
From a distance, unacknowledged legislators
Who derive their powers from chewing bitter leaves
Of a bush that grows outside a bus depot high
Up in the mountains. Snow has piled black and scalding
Over the dark, shapeless masses of barns and farm
Houses. It feels like wolf weather, the awful howls
Of the wind dying away in the dusty crawl
Space under the rafters, the small, pale sun setting
Remotely into encroaching shades of evening.

Dry Lake

In dawn-parched reedbeds quick pale marsh birds take off
    cold
From standing stop, leaping onto thermals like startled
Commuters—self-unseeing suspended motes in
The expansive epiphany of the moment,
Scrawled across the high plateau sky in cirrus streamers

October

Autumn rain falls soundfully from sky to roof, roof to
Pavement. Saturated with leaves, the gutters are blocked.
Drip and trickle, trickle and drop. On the ceiling, first
  imaginal
Discolorations of the inevitable seep and stain. Purposeful
Weeping of Pluvius spreads a soft mist over world,
Remorseful, dully percussive serenade of infinite droplets.

The Drowned Cathedral

The angel asked, as his shoulders were pressed into the
 stone,
Why me? And taken away from the inhabited body,
Like the lyric voice rustling from memory forests,
Childhood rushes toward death, a wind in those woods,
Crashing through trees, dying out,
Settling like a white mist over everything.

Four Cindy Sense-Plays

> "... snatch once in our lives the privilege of arresting the glance of a queen ..."
> —Proust

In the first sequence she wears white clothes, like those in which the dead are buried, and the tawny gold of her skin has a musky odor. In the second she wears black, symbol of mourning among those who survive, and the blond ivory of her flesh gives off a spiky aroma as of camphor, or sandalwood burning. In the third she dresses in violet, the shade of separation, and a burnished darkness hangs over the clarity of her body like a fine, soft fur that's been soaked in and now reeks heavily of gasoline. In the fourth, bathed in mysterious silence, a dark and yet blue sky full of stars curves upward into a thick carpet of black dust that seems to fall slowly and settle in the trembling golden channel of the river, upon which, like slim boats gliding along, arrows of shadow mingle and intersect as they slip forward between shapeless massed growth on banks that, charged with an even more ominous absence of sound, emanate a sharp, clinging odor of must or mildew. Representations of the hours of insomnia of the dying and of statues of mythological figures people have not only ceased to believe in, but perhaps never even heard of, fill the scroll-poems of the beings who live along this river, beings we have come to find but have not yet seen and can now think of only with the same growing foreboding those explorers must have felt, who, having left their homes and the order and safety of their great cities to prove the truth of what the world has so far refused to accept as anything more than mere conjecture, advance deeper and deeper into the possibility that their most trusted suppositions were not only wrong but symptoms of a curious defect of the mind that, like a hairline crack in a mirror, is not apparent until some slight jolt or jar of the factual setting causes the image before one to break up and dissolve into many imperceptible but extremely sharp fragments, each moving outward at a great rate of speed and capable of inflicting great damage. And it is at this point that from the invisible distance there comes a high pitched fluting sound that gradually intensifies until we are able to identify it as the unmistakable tinkling music of Cindy's laughter, perhaps projected over loudspeakers to attract us, as part of a larger general deception whose full scale and details will not become evident until it is too late. We leave the theatre sweat-drenched and shaken, hesitant to speak or even look into one another's eyes. It is only at this point we remember what it is that has brought us here: the fragile but tenacious hope that, despite the commonness of our character and origins, and at whatever cost, we might be able to snatch once in our lives the privilege of arresting the glance of a queen...

Perverse

Bit by bit daily life becomes infinitely perverse. The night begins to have no place for moonlight in it. Walking down streets at the edges of big cities, it seems sometimes pain has a head but not a body. Still we know where our limbs are, and when the sky finally opens, how and why they move.

Message from the Captain

Not much time before landing, might as well say all this at last. A little wrath gave me a place to hide my face in, but when that passed and I looked in the eyes of those I'd left here to wander alone under the low ceiling of an empty sky, mercy measured the extent of my great openness, and I said: I won't say one more word; and I dashed my headset to the cockpit floor.

Nothing mars the clarity of this calm desert night sky until I will it. There's a lot of cloud cover as we go down. The departure of the mountains and the removal of the hills may well ensue, but not the ending of this feeling of deep peace waiting at the end of the landing strip; into which, as on a ship drifting after being wrecked in a storm, one must belatedly and unexpectedly happen. I think I can make out the runway lights.

Departure Air Miracle

The japonaiserie of bay and islands
In the long rush of January storms
About six o'clock I take out my guitar
The moment turned inside out opens

Life moves the blood again, the veins are warm
The moon bathes nude in the thin cloud foam
Making ordinary landscapes appear fractured
Under the blue ceiling of an empty street

A sky full of sparks eliminates shadows
All night a boat swings as if to sink
The body of this thought must be a star
And time passes by, changing nothing

Saeta

Possessed by phantom touch in deep blue
Stardust of a cold winter dusk
I am tuned in to your power station
Airborne at illumination hour
Soprano sax sounds float seaward
Over East Bay hills' heavy green shoulders
Drawn by dark earth rising plants
I hold on to night's rich mane
Like some buffalo soldier on an Indian pony
As black clouds mass over the Sierra

The Astronomer

Well, they are gone and I am alone
In my lime green plum tree bower laughing place.
Where are they now, under a cold heaven
Grown wide with September's dusky light

Through which a giant Steller's jay
Gliding out of the lower tiers of a redwood
Beats its brilliant path homeward—now a fat
Blue blur flashing, now vanishing in light?

Identity quizzer, did you see them go?
Oracle of my lonerhood, weren't you
Taking names? It's a little like a Greek
Play, isn't it?—A sulky hero's central

Wonderment and confusion as he bobs
In the iron palms of that inept
Juggler, fate. Soon to land on hard ground
In an indecorous plot, how do you

Know who walks beside you—the blue-eyed stand-in
Who is your understudy, or yours truly,
Skulking dwarfly off to view imagined stars
Which burn amid the dark plum branches?

Big Boss

Big bossy Steller's jay lets out
its critical view of doings
of quite dimwitted squirrel who
arrives to interrogate the earth
under the plum tree for the nth
time: buried nut there in previous
life? Would love to speak your language.
O easier philosopher,
I'd learn to confer with birds and
trees. But Nature's mystick Book, shut
up on Caliban's dusty shelf,
keeps its bright secrets to itself.

Excalibur

While the new moon winter bright swimming
Up overhead holds the old moon cradled
In its lap like a baby whose augury
Is not its coy smile but the dancing
Lights that play continually across
Darkening hints of menace in its eyes,
This peculiar tint of yellow green
In the still serene and balmy western sky
Spills into that starless lake of blue
To the east like a glass of chartreuse

Poured into a deep vat of ink. Well!
If the bard was weatherwise who made
That grand old ballad of Sir Patrick Spens
A meteorological talisman,
We'll wake up to a storm before morning
Ineradicably closes in on us
Its dark umbrella of probability,
But is that really cause for celebration
Any more than dreams that end short of climax
And appear to promise so much more than they give?

Heraldic Emblem

Circling on his nervous white horse
Through outer perimeter trees
That form the pale of our defense,

Staying equidistant always
From our vulnerable outpost,
A black knight has us on his mind.

Time crawls. Bright glints of shield and lance
From the treeline return our fears
To us in the impatience of

That masked, unforgiving rider,
Illusion of a presence all
These frightened histories project.

Emotions of the moment are
Windows in the castle of fact
Whose solid dimensions appear in

The forest of mirrors out there
To answer such vague reflections
With a blunt certainty of stone.

Interrogative Reflection

What's the burden of this melancholy? Mind?
Within these bones what rankle is assigned
And who assigned it, in what ancient place?
What rage is this? What furor of what kind
Pursues futility back to square root,
Shinnies the tree, neglects to pick the fruit,
Forgets the maiden tied to the railroad tracks,
Recalls the game, yet given chance to choose
Between two cards passes up the ace,
Plays the joker, pretends a poker face,
Yet as next card issues from the dealer's hand
Is caught showing false grin mixed with menace?

Better Days

Once, so it seemed, Fortune threw long
Arms around my neck and kissed me.
What can I have had on my mind
When I made the mistake of not
Suspecting this impossible?

No one can have back ancient pasts
To rearrange for convenience
Of these presents. Trust's to the self
Deceived what paint was to the old
Masters, with the accent on *old*,

Though as everybody believes
What they most want to believe will
If it comes true somehow save them
In the end strange things must happen
To those who do too much thinking.

Mahler's Third

The tonal brightness of a post horn blown
By a Pan whose contempt for us is open
Heralds the betrayal of trust theme,
A clarity undermined by suspicion.

Drop by drop time wears out fate, the way hearts
Are double crossed by thoughts. The forest
Is large and there are so many paths, Lord
Help the traveler who hazards here alone.

Still there is not yet reason to despair:
All is well though in fact all could be lost.
Reluctantly the sun breaks through.
You stir in your sleep, perhaps dream-troubled.

Out of a pale canopy of Teutonic sky
Once supported by compliant lances
Knights held in fealty to forest lords
Rain falls, the floor of time grows slippery

As cold marble a metaphysician
Deep in big thought paces, battering his head
Against the brick wall of the stifling
Inability of language to speak.

A tree creaks at the edge of the wood.
The sun is gone. Under the spreading shade
Of some offence a veil of false tears falls;
Soon all these things will become clearer.

The Burden

The erotic monotone of the night
Condenses into a boat that sinks beneath
A young couple's weight as they make love
Late at night on the small pond or lake
Of the amusement park, which by day is set
Aside for sailing of toy yachts by children
On whom the great weight of love has not yet dropped.

Overhead stars fall like snow. Beneath the hull
Patient weeds feel all about their undinal
Home, waving and moving everywhere
Without ever making progress. Gentle
Throbbing of water like a metronome
Against the oarlocks tosses the boat
And its passengers into eternity.

Let us steer that becalmed boat back ashore,
Pry those lovers from one another's arms, slash
A black line across the lake and the night,
Cancelling out the dream of romance, with its
Rocking vectors of attraction and recoil.
Too soon Monday morning will come, compelling
Youth down into reality's steel grasp.

Early Tudor Court Poems

From the Book of Balettes

Blow, northern wind, come back centuries late,
Wrong person, wrong time, stranger at the gate
Bids farewell, in chill moonlight walks off west,
Freshness of primal world's cold white moon
Peals like clear voice to tingling stars in
Exultant answer to unasked question,
As flames of Yule log flicker on hearth viewed
Through window from rugged hills far off,
Where traveler pauses to listen to the wind,
Imagines unseen carolers in the night,
Makes out snatches of forgotten song
He'd dance to gladly if he but knew the tune.

Pastimes of the Early Tudor Court

What is love? Opportunity
pushes the hot wind down hill
side, tinder in its path invites
casual foxhole fire to strike.

On dry days a man might hunt.
On wet days the fun of throwing
arrows over a screen, or bowls
toward a jack, could soon get old.

Men turned to that more engaging
game that gambled with true risk, caught
a swift glance, garnered a quick kiss,
saw an adventure to be tried,

and wagered everything on it.

Siege Mentality

In early Tudor court's seemingly endless
Tournament of deceiving and being
Deceived, honor to the code and salvation
Of one's skin draw opposing brackets.
Reciprocity of affection
Knocks secrecy off its dark horse,
Leaving love and loyalty in double
Jeopardy: clanging mail, saddle sores
And the machinations of those hooded
Riders whose nervous pacings around
Our encampment suggest all this tension
Is the objective correlative of love
Thudded into by siege engine from hell.

Rondeau

Were they cousins? Had they
Before they were ever lovers
Been friends as children,
    So long ago?

While she sat and sewed
Did he sing and play
Such tunes as came to him
From old lays of service
    Sung long ago?

Was she the fair falcon
In his epigram on luck
That lying pale on the wind
Brought favor to him
Before he was forsaken
    So long ago?

Dizzy Minstrel

For it is out of some book of
Old balettes, where you wear your heart
Upon your sleeve and feeling's allowed
To spoil the game not until first

Lightheaded moment passes, deeper
Accents of emotion come back,
And laying lute and song book down,
He lets his head fall in his hand,

His elbow to rest on oak table,
While breath of happiness swiftly glides
Updraft away, and cold shadow falls
Over Lady Greensleeves' laughter.

The Case

While she sits and sews the needle pricking
Her finger shifts its sting to him withal.
He throws the blame on the lady and
Accuses love of an aversion to him.

Torturing himself to madness he founds
Claim of recompense solely on time spent
And sweat wasted in service sans reward,
Arguing love's case as a thing rational,

The basis of a theory of rights,
As if his suffering were a tax on her heart
But that none of this logic quite applies
Is proven with pricking upon pricking,

For before the sessions of cold fortune
To which appeal to time served means zero
Advocacy of feeling demanding
Affection by love's laws has no case.

Uneasy Passage (October 1532)

Writing on shipboard in rocking channel
Mind spilled now this way now that in long
Rolling pitches of the night and stifled
Thought. Flaring up again of the old love/hate
Debate. *Sometime I fled the fyre that me brent.*
A long slow wave lifts the ship, stops thinking
And holds it in the air a moment before settling.
Anne and her blind King in the royal cabin,
Doing what fate has caused them to be doing.
Wyatt of two minds. Unwilling embassy
Accompanying Anne and her doting
Caesar to Calais, discovering desire spent
Once out of England again as of late
Upspringing, too heated, inconvenient
And not easily suppressed: *And now*
I follow the coles that be quent
From Dovor to Calais, against my mynde.

Poet-Ambassador

Compromised, unblinded, yet still loyal
To the code of service—a professional
Diplomat limited by amateur's rules—
With Bonner now hounding his every move
He followed Carlos from Madrid to Flanders.

He went back into the court of France.
Hoping as in the game of bowls he'd played
With the King when both were enamored of Anne
To help out Harry, whether Harry took leave
From shagging to pick up the point or no,

He tipped François to Carlos' arrogant goad;
And when the French queen countered does he think he's
God? laughed but dwelt within on his own master
The way radiation contemplates its sun,
And kept his feelings to himself in his dispatches.

Maid in Waiting at the Court of Venus

The fate of one young girl of nineteen
May look like a moon pulled toward its sun
With the compulsion of a sudden flood
Wherein the wild river seeks its arroyo
And the breaking out of nature as king

To spill danger across the abstract
Ivory mesas of a barren chessboard
Of power is terrible and absolute
As the May goddess' coldly transfixing
Green eyes, condemning and defining her

But if from here we look again we see
Her mistress of her own body mastering
The arts of possessing others', so skin
Tight hold on her of history loosens,
And distance lights up her own eyes for us

Apples (February 1533)

Her black eyes flashing with appetite
Bred of sudden power, Anne swept in
On a wave of happy laughter—
And "without rhyme or reason amidst great company"
As the Spanish ambassador reported
Declared to the nonplussed Wyatt a furious
Hankering these three days to eat apples
Such as she had never had in her short
Sweet life before—entirely convincing
As she said her hopeful (and foolish,
Her laughing eyes added) new lover the King
She was with child, when in fact no such thing
Was the case—she laughed again, black eyes alight,
"Lord! I wish I had an apple—for
Three days now I have a mad desire
To eat apples"—and whirled out, leaving
Him and everyone in the room stunned
This just after the secret wedding and
A few months before the fatal coronation.

Anticipation

In that month devoted to observances
Of Venus, when everyone whispered at once
In nervous panic under stairs, by candle light
Long silences fell, hysteria ran among the maids,
Who was then betrayer, who betrayed?
The net drawing about them all awakening
Its filaments in everyone's raw nerves
The night passed in hushed respiration
Of still listening hearts, as nightingales
Sang outside to the tingling stars
And bright morning found men lying
In bed dreaming in mischance, recalling
Haps the most unhappy that ever did befall.

Turnabout

Anne's blurting out to Kingston her keeper
In the Tower that Wyatt had blown or
Whistled on his fist against her forges
Another link in the chain of perfidy
And mutual betrayal. Wyatt has once
Loved her, and maybe she him, yet too when
Posed with the fact of the King's interest
He has offered to arrange that he and
She be witnessed by the Privy Council
In flagrante delicto. Once he blows on
His fist to save his head hers is as good as off.

Wyatt in the Tower (May 1536)

Adding up his offense against her disdain
He put his case: simple compensation,
His suit to sustain, expenditure stated,
Such and such paid out in bitter tears, shame,
Forfeiture of trust, with loss of good name
Consequent upon disgrace, and now this
Involuntary vigil upon deaths
Of fellows in misfortune of ill use
Compounding the sum of favor love owed
If its debt to all were to be charged—
A computation devised to pass away
Anxious hours awaiting his own judgment
While over hill bell tolled for each accused
Lover sans remorse five strokes one per head.

Month of Venus (May 1536)

> *the bell towre showed me suche syght*
> *that in my hed stekys day and nyght*

Wyatt, recruited into his
Lord the King's school of hard knocks,
Already *in mornyng wyse* in
This black, bloody month of Venus,
Two long slow nights since Tower bell
First tolled over hill from his cell,
Hears heavy bolts move in locks,
Keys jangle dully on a ring,
Steps drag large weight up stair well
Out of thick darkness, fear-charged
Medium in which something bright
Sinks, while something unspoken swims
Snakelike, muddy oil-yellow eyes,
Russet scales on slick sides glinting.

Dawn breaks in a red stain seeping
Upward into a mother of
Pearl bowl. Friday 19 May. Poet's
Hands that in tourney with the King
Gripped a lance grasp iron grates'
Continuing hard instruction.
Queen Anne, a net of pearls holding
Up her dark hair in lost crown's place,
Wearing robe of dovegrey damask
Cut low after the style of the court,

Sable trimmed, with crimson kirtle,
Comes down the little prepared green,
Climbs a single low wooden stair
Up to the long straw-strewn platform.

Last Act

Speaks her little speech, fidgets, looks
Back quickly at the hulking man
With the two-handed sword who stands
Over her shoulder to one side,
Kneels down like a girl, has her eyes
Bound by matrons, and while still in
The act of crying out to some
Absent deity for pity
Has her head severed from her trunk,
The former rolling on the straw
Then thrown into and along
With the latter trundled off in
What looks to the thunder struck
Wyatt like a long arrow box.

History

Anne had no defense against the shrinking
Box of history, and as the walls closed,
Suddenly no one she knew seemed to know
Her, she'd shrunk so small no one could see her,
As if embarrassed the knights and ladies
Looked away, so that when like a tree
Falling in a forest heard by no one
The hard blade collided with her slender neck,
Completing the reduction of her to zero,

None of it would be so much as noticed
By anyone, except through prison grates
And bitter tears by Wyatt, who could not
Help but watch, and those curious women
Of the city who, hanging out their wash,
Turned silently to look up at the sky,
And boatmen on the Thames, lying on their oars,
And looking toward the Tower, heard cannon boom
And as the heavy sound rolled through space

Many a citizen of the town stood still
Listening to the silence in the wake
Of that solitary detonation—she with
Bowl lifted under arm, he with gesture
Arrested, adze or mallet lifted as if
In mimicry of the headman's weapon,
Did not need anyone to tell them the meaning
Of this sign, or construe the name
Of who it is that around thrones thunders.

Luckes, my faire falcon

White falcon on the wing outsoars the dark
Trajectory of her fate, then falls back
To float and drift on warm airs of spring.
Does her story have to come out tragic?
Courtly cloudburst without shade of warning:
In her transition from ritual to rue
Anne Boleyn learned crowns could come with all
That pain, then be taken back again,
Power's revolving potlatch without proof
Any providence is in control
Or even witnesses what simply happens.

Her Revisitation

He falls again in that unstable
Dream according to place varied
In which the restless captive frets
In the falcon cage of power

Through the pitches of the night
Tossing and turning, broad waking
Awaiting her ghost revenant
And back she comes night after night

Lithe wraith out of that old tempest
As a sprite to tempt, then leap back
Into fire's immaterial
Mutation: him in a cold sweat

Twisting agitated covers
In his hands like a man trying
Without success to tear up
The manuscript of his death warrant

Withdrawal

Skating over the slippery top of court
Estates having induced in him a great
Yearning to live unseen and unheralded
And use me quyet without lett or stoppe,
Unknowen in courte that hath such brackishe ioyes,
Withdrawal from the scene started to look good
To Wyatt, and in hindsight who can blame him,
Knowing what we know about the House of Fame,
Its many mansions one upon another,
For he who with the Other is acquainted
But to himself dies unknown, dazed with
Dreadful face, death grips like a yeoman
Who grabs a fowl hard by the crop and snaps
Its neck with a sound familiar at court.

House Arrest

Clerk of policy tutored at boot of that
Royal killer who Luther said meant to
Be God, and do what he pleased with everyone,
Wyatt spent his years of knighthood falling
In and out of arms of women and nations—
Loyalty to old codes of service fading
To sickness at heart, duty become bleak job.

That quiet interval of exile into
Kent some months or years before the end,
Marks of manacles still smarting,
Out of the Tower, bound by force of disdain,
Whether leashed unto his father's charge in
House arrest, or on his own recognizance,
Is the one hint of mercy in the story,

And that not quite plain. Did his liberty
Contain freedom of choice? Though surveilled
Was he free to move? History blindly
Clutching at fact in dark of all that's been finds
Him claiming content at home to hunt and hawk
Or in foul weather with book to sit, in frost
And snow with bow to stalk though slow time drags.

Combustion (Katheryn Howard & Henry VIII)

It was Katheryn's intercession
Saved Wyatt from the Tower,
True loyalty to their small
Circle of poetry loving
Lovers and friends, revolving
About and drawing energy
From and greatly fearing Henry:
Quick with mischief and vivacity,
Making air almost sizzle around her,
Still she was scarcely the delightful
Toy the King surmised. Brightest
And freshest of the brilliant
Waterflies of his court, she had,
Pursued around and through the flame,
Emerged with singed wings, though
Her sweet and abundant nature,
Invigorating temper, love of joy,
And impulse to give of herself rather
Than to acquire, had concealed the burn
At first. The past, however, is hard
To shed in a blackmailing world.

The Fall of Katheryn Howard

Impolitic text of the past unfolding
In a chain of tales whispered down dimly
Lit corridors and under kitchen stairs,
Quite quickly all her indiscretions
Came to the bleak light of that cold killing
Season, and all the old grudges aired
Out a history in which love had found
Her "in arms kissing," and haunted her
Bedchamber nightly in the entirely
Credible persons of some several
Alert, opportunistic young men,
During long, love-making, murmuring,
Bickering, promising, reproaching,
Passionate English summer evenings.

The Collector

To him she was a jewel of womanhood
He had, though ageing, luckily lighted on
As if he had brought home a treasure in
Faience. But to her he was less man
Than circumstance, all enveloping
Proprietariness: what he desired
Yet could not possess completely could
Not be allowed to continue to live.
But she did not know this, nor that
His inability to own her entire
History would so inflame desire
As to aggravate him unto that
State of rage and confusion which could
Be relieved only by removing her head.

The Blushing Rose

The "blushing rose without a thorn"
Her love-blind gross prince saw was
In fact a fair and forward young
Thing with an eye for handsome cavaliers:
Into the depths of her cheerfulness
He plummeted her death.
Her acceptance of her fate
Was half brave, half insensate.
She had not given herself to her
Accused lovers as often perhaps
As was thought, but wished to have,
And taking the consequences of
Her dishonesty, she proved true
To her conscience, so that on a cold
Candlemas, with the trees bare,
The stars hardly gone out, and the air
Wraithed with mists that spoke
Of the nearness of the Thames, she
Went trembling to the block, bent her neck,
The headsman swung, and out gushed
Her young blood in a terrible torrent
That clotted on and clung to the black
Cloth in which her little headless body
Was wrapped, lifted up and swiftly borne
Off to be buried in the chapel of
St. Peter de Vincula alongside
The remains of her cousin Anne Boleyn.

Impalpable

What can it be like to have in lost time
Lived, loved, been such cunning brave proud sensitive
Frightened conniving secretive tale telling
Persons: as real as you and me yet
Compressed by great weight of history into
Slim ghosts flitting nervously under and through
Locked doors of an impalpable past.

Confessions

Dowsing

"He was a thoroughly delightful man, when sober," my cousin Jim says of his uncle Bud, Arthur Clark, my father. Jim has researched family history in recent years, and much of what I know about the earlier generations of my father's family comes from him. But though my dad was the youngest of four children and an early darling, seemingly favored by fate and certainly much loved then and later by the two older sisters who survived him, something in him went terribly wrong, and that wrong-going, in retrospect, looks increasingly less like an accident or aberration than the sad expression of some ingrained canker in the blood. What makes some people not fit into the world that surrounds them? Is it just that they don't like feeling so surrounded?

An older brother of my father's, John Clark, a quiet, serious man who was said to spend a lot of time reading, appears in one poor reproduction of a family photo I've seen. In a dark suit, gravely handsome, enigmatic, unsmiling, he stands in the center of the back row, the tallest figure in the photo (my father, looking about thirteen at the time, always the most "outgoing," smiles winningly at the camera from down in front). Next to my uncle John in the back row stands the head of the family, Willard Clark, itinerant sign painter, veteran of the Great War, jaunty in a boater, with a cocked grin, worldly, dapper-looking. Seated in a chair before Willard is his plump, dark-haired wife, Irene née Cann—daughter of Mary Burke, an immigrant girl who'd been born in steerage, arriving orphaned in the New World (both a twin sister and her mother had died at sea), and of the equally unfortunate John Cann, who'd entered America from Nova Scotia just in time to serve with the Illinois

Volunteers in the Civil War and lose his right arm at Peach Tree Creek, Georgia ("They gave him a shot of whiskey and sawed it off"). A year or two after this backyard Chicago family-gathering photo was taken, Willard, my second namesake—I would be called Thomas Willard—was dead. By then his two daughters had married, leaving the two sons alone with their mother.

My dad left high school and went to work, while his brother John stayed at home. One day Bud walked into the house and found their mother stricken on the kitchen floor with a sudden catastrophic stroke. He ran for help, but before it came Irene was dead. That was August 1936. The following April there came a further blow, when the quiet, serious, book-reading older brother took his own life by walking east into Lake Michigan until his hat floated. (Not to make too much of it, but to my knowledge my father never swam. Our few family vacations to the Wisconsin lake country, to me a land of F. Scott Fitzgeraldian mythic glamor, were short and unhappy. I remember him taking me fishing once or twice in leaky rented rowboats; that was clearly an ordeal for him. Of course back then I couldn't have guessed why. I didn't learn about my uncle's suicide until many, many years later—just recently, in fact; all through my life at home that suicide remained a shameful, painful secret, unknown not only to me but to my younger brother John, who was named after that unfortunate man.) My father seems to have spent the rest of his days doggedly dowsing bottle after bottle in search of his own black lake of forgetfulness to wade off into. Had life in this world of surprising, gratuitous cruelty and pain taken off its mask for him at too early an age?

Through one of his sisters who'd married a stockbroker, Bud got a job as a bond trader on the Chicago Exchange, and did well for a time, until the relentless seriousness of his drinking problem reared its vicious head. A good-looking, wavy-haired fellow much favored by the ladies—"quite the collar ad," one of them later recalled him—he dated a pretty, vivacious young Irish-American woman named Rita Kearin, who at the time was working as a shopgirl and living at home after graduating from a west suburban Catholic college. They saw a little of one another, but he seemed to lose interest, and disappeared for some months. Then he was hauled in by the law for drunken driving. To forestall formal charges he showed up, sober and contrite, at the front door of Rita's father, a local police captain. The captain helped him out, and shortly afterwards, in 1939, the quick-witted, fast-talking Buddy married my mother.

Exempted from service in World War II because of high blood pressure, he was put to work at a Douglas Aviation plant located west of the city in raw Illinois countryside later to become O'Hare airport; the DC-3 was then in development, and his draughtsman's skills were employed in helping design it. Those skills had been inherited from his father, the sign painter, though whether his father or anyone else had ever formally instructed him in drawing I don't know. At any rate, he drew with a strong, bold, flowing line. (He taught or anyway inspired me to draw, too—an avocation absorbing enough to earn me many a brisk rap across guilty knuckles from ruler-brandishing nuns irritated by my inattention in religion and arithmetic classes.) Later on he continued to make use of this gift, as and when he could. That was, however, only marginally. He made silk screens and decals for a while, and as a hobby did decorative art, sometimes of remarkable quality; I recall his movie-star-caricature wall-murals done for the basement barroom of the South Oak Park house of his stockbroker brother-in-law, where we later lived (by then, like other forgotten reminders of his once-promising future, they'd long since been painted over). In his last days as an invalid, when drinking had destroyed his health, he took up his old oils to turn out knock-off Renoirs and Van Goghs on wooden trivets, to be sold in his sister's interior-decorating showrooms. Considering his diminished circumstances, even these rather kitschy late productions were surprisingly competent. Then again, they represent the sad testament of a wasted talent.

In his middle years, the years of his heaviest drinking, before a series of strokes confined him to the house, he went through a series of increasingly depressing traveling salesman's jobs, peddling first decals, then later cans and cardboard boxes for a number of different firms. I remember riding along with him at age nine or ten on one midsummer box-selling junket across the Mississippi into Iowa. We stopped at John Deere and International Harvester farm equipment plants in hot, dusty nowhere burgs like Moline and Davenport, whose mundane Midwestern ordinariness did not dim their electrifying away-from-home aura for me, and spent a night at the Blackhawk Hotel in Des Moines, where the Indian murals in the dining room convinced me I'd finally entered the fabled territory of the West—I remember being quite excited about that. However, I also remember my father's tenseness and jumpiness throughout the trip. The dingy, unromantic traveling salesman's life, worse than Arthur Miller ever conceived it, was my father's professional reality. While being good at thinking on his feet when sober helped him land salesman's job after salesman's job, selling inevitably made him hate not only those he had to sell to but himself, and in the long run contributed no little to his ultimate humiliation. He seldom held *any* job very long; as the years went by and his range narrowed, he drank more and more, and finally seemed to leave his paycheck in West

Madison Street bars far more often than he showed up at home with it.

As my father's sharp wit grew dull with progressive alcohol poisoning, and a general sense of bitterness and disappointment overcame his natural charm, the bloom of life was taken away from my mother in predictable proportion, till all pretense to domestic harmony buckled under the strains of their unfortunate union. From the turmoil and damage of life at home, my own sole secure refuge came to be that provided in my maternal grandfather's relatively much happier household. Accordingly, I spent longer and longer periods of time there, relieved to be safely away from the violent battleground of home and increasingly reluctant to return to it.

My parents aside, perhaps the most important person in my early life was Thomas Patrick Kearin, my mother's father, on whose birthday (March 1) I came into the world, and whose first name I was accordingly given. A hale, robust young man from a large family whose origins lay in the romantic Gaelic-speaking wilds of County Kerry on Ireland's southwest coast (he retained a strong west-country brogue throughout his life), he'd come down around the turn of the century to Chicago from South Dakota, striking out on his own in the roughneck city of that era, first as a street lamplighter, then as a streetcar driver, before settling into his life's work as a policeman. A physically imposing man, he possessed also great energy, and a cheerful Celtic goodheartedness and generosity exceptional even in a race noted for those traits. In 1912 he married a tiny, pert young Irish girl named Kathleen Gaynor, a pub keeper's daughter and telegraph operator from the crossroads town of Mullingar in County Westmeath, who'd emigrated at age eighteen in order to avoid an arranged marriage. My grandfather devoted himself thenceforth to an extended family that soon included not only his and Kathleen's two daughters but seven of his own eight siblings, who'd also landed in America, as well as his mother and father. When his parents' health failed in the 1920s, he personally fetched them home from California in dutiful Old Country fashion to take their final rest in his own house. I have a photo of his father, Humphrey Kearin, laid out amid flowers in the front room of that Harlem Avenue house in Oak Park, and my mother recalls quite vividly as one of the most affecting events of her own girlhood the traditional Irish wake afforded there to her grandmother Johanna Horan Kearin. It was an event of nightlong drinking, dancing and storytelling—a kind of mourning, as she is still moved to remember it, that seemed not so much woeful grieving as joyful lamentation, the communal celebration of a life valued in its passing. Indeed that same house at Harlem and Augusta remains the site of many of my own happiest early memories: a tree-shaded homestead, adjacent to daisy-filled fields and woods (all paved concrete and suburban development now); also to the western arterial thoroughfare of Harlem Avenue, and, a little farther off, the Chicago & North Western railroad tracks, sources of those nocturnal sounds of long-distance truck tires and train whistles that to my dreamily listening ears, as I lay awake late at night in the upstairs bedroom, summoned vistas of wide-open prairies beyond.

    By the time I got to know him, my grandfather was already a man of broad experience that ranged from seeing action in the line of duty at the scene of the St. Valentine's Day Massacre to busting up beer and whiskey barrels in the streets during Prohibition. While enforcing the Volstead Act was professionally required of him, he remained himself no disrespecter of the good uses of an occasional glass of spirits, and whether or not it's just my imagination, the news photo I have of him in plainclothes supervising the destruction of a bootlegger's haul seems to indicate, only partially concealed beneath his straw boater, a look of mild dismay over the unfortunate waste involved.

Prominent among my childhood memories of him are those involving the protracted festivities of Christmases in his household, a time when a veritable magic bounty of tribute invariably arrived from his grateful constituency, the doorbell steadily ringing with messenger deliveries "for the Chief," fat turkeys by the dozen, potted poinsettias, hand-packed boxes of fancy fruit and nuts from the Pacific Northwest (a place I imagined as a remote forested factory of spectacular benisons), an annual year's supply of Mars Bars and Eskimo Pies (the sheer plentitude of which, along with the turkeys, required two large basement freezers to contain them), and, most notable of all to my childish eyes, a cornucopia of cases of fine bourbon, generously offered to seasonal visitors for convivial social consumption. The climax of this mysterious torrent of gifts was of course Christmas morning, when my grandfather always left out a shot of bourbon for Santa Claus, and I myself without fail rose hours before all others to hungrily attack my own small treasure-trove of gifts. One year, I'm informed—I must have been about three or four—my great joy over some wooden racing cars I'd been given spilled over into a misguided attempt to share it by opening up everyone else's packages too, and painting the contents with red nail polish, a task I was able to accomplish just in time for the rest of the family to walk in and find their presents coated with a wild crimson lacquer.

My grandfather, who'd never had a son of his own, lavished vast transferred paternal indulgence on me; on this occasion, as on all too many others subsequently, he warded off any possible criticism of my excessive deed with the injunction, "Just give the lad another month." He was always ready to forgive me anything. One winter when I was in seventh or eighth grade I was caught—and for good measure, cuffed around by the civic-minded juice-truck driver who'd caught me—tossing snowballs into a mail van; beat cops who were summoned had no choice but to haul me into the station house, where my grandfather's discomfort was so evident I for once actually regretted my transgression. He attempted to demonstrate my innocence to his bemused police cronies by having me exhibit my gloves, which he claimed were dry as a bone even though they were obviously caked with ice from furious snowball-making.

Just how far his protection may have extended beyond the bounds of his beloved family to other interests always remained a matter of some question to me. At the borders of that shadow of a doubt, just across Harlem Avenue in the neighboring village of River Forest, a number of alleged crime bosses were known to make their homes—some, like the notorious Tony Accardo, in plush mansions with rolling lawns, tennis courts, ballrooms and bowling alleys, some in abodes that were at least to the casual eye much more modest. One of the more discreet reputed-mobster domiciles was in fact visible from my grandfather's front-window easy chair, into which, putting up his big pearl-handled pistol out of child's reach and whistling a few bars of some old Killarney ballad, he settled for his daily noontime "forty winks." How much he knew or didn't know about the secrets that lay behind those shuttered windows across the Avenue I of course can't know, but considering that as early as 1946 he'd risen to the position of chief of the Oak Park police force, I'd guess he knew quite a bit. Of those particular neighbors, anyway, he spoke with the wry distance of someone who appeared relieved to have them outside his jurisdiction. When I was in high school with the family's scion, a pleasant enough fellow whose well-oiled ducktail and pegged slacks declared his membership in a "hoody" set that definitely was not mine, a nightclub in an adjacent town unaccountably burned down one evening just before a school prom had been scheduled to occur there. That nightclub had moreover been selected as prom site over the objections of the son of my grandfather's Italian-American neighbor, who'd held out for another establishment to which his family was speculated to have a more than passing connection.

Indeed there sometimes seemed to be invisible sympathies and affiliations, unspoken connections and dependencies, locked into place almost everywhere in this primordial landscape, at once silently sustaining and implicitly inhibiting. Social as well as religious understandings in our little corner of the world were based not so much on the cold relations of logic as on more emotional or imaginative ones of faith and trust, often requiring irrational leaps as a matter of course. These were in many respects a hardheaded as well as hard-working people, yet a certain semi-mystical suspension of disbelief generally prevailed. On my mother's side of the family, superstitions were commonplace, including but not limited to an orthodox Catholic credence in miracles. Irish folk wisdom did little to separate the available mythologies in this regard. My grandmother had brought over with her from the Old Country a stereopticon in whose binocular viewer one could glimpse hand-tinted misty twilit Celtic copses where strange "little people" wandered the gloaming, doing the supernatural things little people were presumed to do. The legendary kingdom of these diminutive fairy beings both intrigued and scared me. For all I could tell, in my youthful unknowingness, the same stretched time-space envelope roamed by the little people also contained, to cite just two among a thousand instances, such places as that spooky grotto at Lourdes where Saint Bernadette, played by the somewhat inappropriately sexy Jennifer Jones in a Hollywood movie we were shown every year by the nuns, had witnessed the Virgin striking water from the rocks; or those unearthly North Polar zones where, according to the theories of an oddball Irish Catholic soft-water magnate whose pamphlet on the subject received great currency in our parish during the cold war's fearful early stages, a continuous series of aurora borealis displays had begun to signal the incipient fulfillment of the promised eschatology of the biblical Abomination of Desolation. The Apocalypse was soon to erupt in the form of global thermonuclear conflict, it was commonly thought. At school, we curled up in practice fetal poses beneath our desks, and at home, blankets were tacked up over the basement windows in dry-run exercises aimed at preparing us for avoiding blinding from the flash of the blast.

In my earlier, even more impressionable years, when a hot war I knew of only through the fraught tones of adults' conversation still raged on in Europe and the Pacific, I was plagued by secret anxieties about something or someone hiding in my bedroom closet after the lamp went out; lights shifted and flickered outside our South Austin Boulevard tenement apartment window, shadows crawled across the walls, and words inexplicably lost their meanings. What was in that closet? A ghost? A "dirty Nazi"? How could I know, I'd never seen one. All too often in those first years of my life I was bedridden with assorted illnesses, and it seems fever too acted as a kind of solvent of meaning, sending me swirling into a vertigo of lost sense. The first movie I recall,

The Spiral Staircase, was one I probably should not have been taken to: all my concealed fears and phobias were confirmed and afterwards ran amok in uncontrolled visions of dangers hidden in dark places; like the deaf-mute heroine in the film, I could neither be sure of the grounding of my private terrors in any tangible reality, nor find words to utter them. I suppose all of this is perfectly normal personality development in certain respects, the predictable problems of adjustment any child experiences in coming to terms with a world that is at least in part a place of unintelligible and inexpressible menace.

Across Austin Boulevard from the large brown brick apartment house that was my first home lay a Chicago city park with scrubby woods and public golf links—Columbus Park, *terra incognita* of my earliest psychic geographizing. In the beginning it was forbidden territory. The tree-shaded landfill hillock with cinder path that ran parallel to the boulevard, defining the park's western boundary, was the supposed lair of unpleasant characters who lurked in wait to snare any insouciant children happening past. Though "God only knew" exactly what these bogeymen did to their victims, one suspected the adults had a clue but weren't telling. Once permitted out on my own, of course, I spent as much time there as possible, foraging with pals through the patchy foliage beside the dandelion-pocked fairways, surreptitiously scavenging lost golf balls and then peddling them back to the golfers for a dime apiece, nicked or waterlogged ones going for a nickel. This was, I believe, the first mercantile enterprise in which I ever took part.

My father had been an excellent golfer in his youth. I have a photo of him, at age thirty-one, holding his driver, lined up in a row with three other local amateur champs, all of them much older than he, taken on the occasion of the

Evanston Rodeo Tournament at Evanston Country Club on the North Shore in the summer of 1942. That was before he'd lost the job as a bond trader—perhaps the peak moment of his hopes in life. Though drinking has already begun to bloat his face in this photo, there is still intelligence in the wide-set, curiously penetrating eyes. But it is the intelligence of someone who's seen the darker side of himself, the face of a man to whom damage is on its way to happen. When I was about ten he gave me his old clubs and taught me to play. I have scorecards of some of our ancient rounds on the Columbus Park links—even when I was thirteen and getting stronger, and he was forty-three and in bad shape, the best I could ever do was come within two strokes of him on the nine-hole course. It was the only sport he ever practiced seriously, though he was fairly astute about how baseball was meant to be played, and played it himself with an adeptness that made our occasional games of catch a useful teaching experience for me.

He took me to my first big-league games at Comiskey Park on the city's South Side. These were intense adventures indeed. The car ride through the most infernal neighborhoods I'd so far ever seen was an education in itself; in the broken-glass-littered streets where we parked, aggressive urchins boldly demanded tribute ("Watch your car, fifty cents," they promised, fleeing if you paid—or, if you didn't, hanging around to slash your tires). Then once inside the big old brick ballpark we marched up long dark grandstand ramps for what seemed an endless time until finally and suddenly emerging through a tunnel into the radiantly illuminated, enchanted emerald-green space. The first game I attended, sometime in 1948 or 1949, was a night contest, won by the Yankees 11-8 on the strength of a bases-clearing double in the top of the eighth by a hobbled and ageing but still elegant Joe DiMaggio. The night left me exhausted but exultant, unable to sleep. My father took me to other games now and then, of course not as often as I would have liked. His own grownup's problems prevented his sharing my religious involvement in the game.

Perhaps religious is the wrong term, though. Part hobby, part escape hatch from endarkened household, for me baseball opened up a secret door in the wall to numinous worlds religion promised but never delivered. Before long I was collecting baseball cards with a passion that defied reason. Hanging out at penny candy shops on Harrison Street, waiting for the season's new shipment of cards to come in, I risked the wrath of the nuns, several times getting caught ditching classes—and, on one infamous occasion, Sunday Mass—for the sake of a wafer of cardboard containing the painted figure of Tommy Holmes or Felix Mantilla, Sam Jethroe or Johnny Groth, Eddie Yost or Irv Noren. Along with each packet of cards came several thick powder-coated slabs of sugary pink bubble gum which I dutifully chewed all through my bike-riding and pickup ballgame days, thus contributing directly to the early stages of the erosion of my now long-gone dental apparatus. Some twenty-five or thirty years later, after I'd left home for good, these vast early collections, having done nothing for decades but gather dust in my mother's attic while concurrently also unbeknownst to her gathering increasing monetary value, were taken out by her into the back alley one day and burned with the rest of the trash. These three facts, the third being the crowning consideration, allow my collecting to remain in my mind one of the few instances of pure sacrifice in my life.

From the age of eight or nine onwards, I listened to White Sox games broadcast by "Commander Bob" Elson on

WCFL radio with an intensity of imaginative involvement rarely equalled in my participation, say, as an altar boy at Mass; indeed the two forms of attention were so linked that I felt no qualms about enlisting the latter in the service of the former, often praying through an entire Sunday morning ceremony for a double-header sweep by the Sox, and deliberately fixing my mind, in the moment of receiving the Eucharist upon my tongue, on certain hoped-for achievements of the day by my current favorite player, be it Billy Pierce, Minnie Minoso, or Nelson Fox.

As an adolescent it was one of my great joys to actually get up close to big-league players through the happy chance of picking up work as a ballpark usher. Over three summers I probably worked some three hundred games at Chicago's two major league parks, met many players, had more than a few interesting conversations with them (Dick Stuart, the home-run-hitting "Dr. Strangeglove" first baseman of the Pittsburgh Pirates, once explained to me his philosophy of dealing with the opposite sex, a subject on which I could use all the coaching I could get), and was even several times (thrill!) mistaken for them by autograph seekers, when in my pre- or post-game white-shirt-and-slacks mufti.

Blue Boy in a Green Shade

In that little urban neighborhood of working-class or lower-middle-class pseudo-respectable lace-curtain Irish where I grew up, three categories of human beings were recognized as more or less warily coexisting: churchgoing Catholics, who dwelt within the familiar limits of that invisible social frontier, the parish; non-Catholics, who dwelt on the exotic other side; and the "fallen away," or embarrassed-circumstance ex-Catholics, who, for all the unknowing child could tell, inhabited some shadowy nether-zone of their own, bound in by disillusion, disappointment and private shame.

It was difficult to be sure exactly why anyone might be tempted (or for that matter—who knew?—driven) into falling away. If the first stirrings of puberty brought hints sex must have something to do with it, still these inklings had to await, and rather impatiently at that, any kind of tangible confirmation. College would inevitably provide it. In the meantime, however, the few hundred dollars that had somehow to be found to pay my tuition at a private Dominican high school were likely well-spent, though you'd perhaps have had a hard time putting that fact across to my father. A reluctant Catholic at best, he'd taken up the faith only under duress, in order to enter a matrimonial state that had anyway turned out somewhat less than entirely blissful, and was besides no great admirer of the confident dogmatic wisdom of the priests. (In the Catholic cop-world of his wife's family, he was always a stranger in a strange land, and as the darkness in his nature more and more revealed itself, was increasingly *non grata* there.) My mother, though, insisted. In consideration of the by then already evident unruly aspects of my character, her view in this matter was probably the more sensible. Noted city-wide for its several disciplines— religious, athletic, scholastic—the school did an excellent job not only of keeping potential hard cases like me off the streets and out of reformatories, but also of moving its graduates (all save a very few of them, and not just the small minority of rich kids) on to college. Thus provided a classical education good enough to qualify me for a small scholarship to a Jesuit liberal arts college in Ohio, I found myself faced with the highly desirable prospect of living away from home for the first time.

Hopeful images of Joe College days, footballs falling through the leaves, lasted but a few weeks. My year with the Jesuits turned out to be for the most part strange and lonely. By midwinter I had moved in with an old high school friend from back home, with whom I probably spent more hours in a certain beer joint on Euclid Avenue in Cleveland than I ever put in on studying. Sad and blue, down to my bottom dollar, I learned from an obliging senior—a lieutenant from my ROTC unit, if memory serves—how to twist a wire coat hanger so that it would, upon insertion, retrieve coins from pay phones, thus making possible nightly hours of long-distance sweet-talking with my teenage main squeeze, an Illinois state champion high school butterfly stroker and (naturally) the daughter of a Chicago cop.

In *The Psychopathology of Everyday Life* Freud suggested there are no accidents, and perhaps it is true that someone who gets into so-called accidents throughout life must in some unconscious sense be self-propelled into them. Recklessness, in any case, has more than once been my undoing. Rushing down dormitory stairs one day, I tripped and plunged headlong through a double-pane, wire-reinforced "safety" window, nearly severing my left arm just above the wrist. Long nights in a Cleveland hospital ensued; a generous Italian-American specialist treated me for months without charge, performing a series of skin-graft surgeries. The folks back home never heard a word about any of this. Further difficulties followed. The complications of a romantic liaison with a local high school girl, daughter of a trucking company boss, caused the embarrassment of a series of increasingly late and disorganized arrivals at a daily 8:00 A.M. history class. Then the phone company started making belated inquiries, and school officials began to diplomatically suggest everyone concerned might be better off if this particularly trouble-prone student were to seek a transfer.

At that age there is still a certain feeling of living a charmed life—a delusion further impressed upon me by what happened next, my seemingly serendipitous admission to the University of Michigan. My first collegiate venture had been an utter washout, and probably should have doomed me for life to the drab working-class existence I so dreaded. Instead I found myself actually welcomed by a much larger and more prestigious institution, which would prove not only much better equipped scholastically, but considerably broader in its tolerance of my often noisome presence. At any rate, things worked out somewhat better there. After a final flourish during a brief fling at fraternity life, my determined wild-oat-sowing mercifully gave over to a first demonstration of serious intent to acquire knowledge. Perhaps forcible body-painting on a frosty midnight and the subsequent dousing-with-firehose during pledge-week helped diminish my loyalty to Sigma Chi; certainly I do recall rueful thoughts afterwards upon finding my photo in the house album, naked, wet and shivering, humorously captioned "Blue Boy."

Ann Arbor became for me a place of dark weeping trees under which long solitary night rambles took me down to the New York Central tracks that ran through the sleepy valley of the Huron River. There, one night, I witnessed a violent quarrel between two strangers that spilled from a car onto the shaded railroad embankment and ended—I was certain, from the *in extremis* sounds that issued out of the invisible trees by that unforgetting river—in bloody murder. Sleepless in my deracinated asceticism, I experienced a derangement of the senses made more acute by month after month of living on apples and coffee to stretch my few final dollars, burning the midnight oil, staring at the light bulb in the

205

ceiling fixture while silent snow piled up in the blackness outside. With the belated arrival of spring, an intensity of lilacs burst upon the surprised air. I had been reading Rilke and Wallace Stevens, but when my spooky-normal landlord, a German-American fellow who wore an Elmer Fudd-style hunting cap every day of the year, informed me that he'd known the family of the poet Theodore Roethke, and that Roethke himself had lived in this neighborhood while at the university, I also began to intuit a darker presence underlying the profuse erotic greenness of the late Midwestern spring. The lofty imperatives of Rilke's angels and the sober contemplative clarities of Stevens' snowy evenings gave way briefly to Roethke's muddier psychic landscape, with its ominous inevitabilities, nurturings of womb and birthplace, mushy, loamy oozings of life-throes circling back to the dark closure of grave-humus. Then I found Boris Pasternak's *Safe Conduct*. Pasternak's testament to another kind of virid lyric springtime—a prism through which the life of poetry appeared such a delicate yet powerful thing, trembling with its singular impossible demand for grace—seemed the most resonant of all.

The poets of the university circuit who came through Ann Arbor, however, were hardly my idea of role models. A recent Pulitzer Prize winner and college-circuit darling of the moment from the Iowa Writer's Workshop read his famous "confessional" lyrics, then at the compulsory professors' party afterward keened disconsolately on a freezing sidewalk during a blizzard. I'll never forget seeing him there on his hands and knees weeping melodramatically into the driving snow—feet clad only in lightweight loafers meant for gently treading fallen leaves, index finger hooked into a Chianti bottle—and remarking inwardly on the tendency of poets to act out the *personae* of their work in public.

The poet of the Library of Congress, a hulking crew-cut Southerner, former Air Force bomber pilot and successful advertising man, came through to do a reading just a few weeks after the appearance in *The New York Times* of an essay he'd penned about the heavy spiritual toll and sincere Platonic satisfactions of being a touring campus poet. From his reaction at the post-reading party to my enthusiastic comments about the new Grove Press anthology of "alternative" poets, I sensed he regarded me as a rather dubious character—and not just because a knee in the groin had been his disappointing reward for following my girlfriend, a diminutive but feisty New Yorker, upstairs to a bedroom and falling upon her atop a pile of coats.

Indeed such opportunities for up-close viewing of the "major" American poets of the day left me with a strong and lasting negative impression. I now look back on this as unfortunate, not so much because I presumed judgment as because, once offered the chance some four or five years later to become a university poet myself (at Iowa, among other proffered places), I turned it down, thus irrevocably exiting, with a headstrong lack of foresight surely to be regretted, the moving staircase of academic poetry-careering. Once you step off that escalator-to-a-secure-mediocrity, you can never step back on.

Meanwhile, of course, Ann Arbor proposed not just poetry's but quite a few other possible voices and ways of life. On the Diag, the open space in front of Rackham Library that served not only as heavily traveled pedestrian thoroughfare but informal center of campus political activity, *soi-disant* radicals, mostly from New York and Chicago, gathered to hear speakers who stood on large stone benches to debate the urgent issues of the hour. I heard a smart, intense, pimply-faced young student politician named Tom Hayden debate Fulton Lewis, Jr. about civil rights, on those benches once, and, another time, a rousing speech by Martin Luther King. Ramblin' Jack Elliott came through town, camped under a tree adjacent to the Diag to pick and sing for his next meal, and included in his repertoire the first Woody Guthrie and Bob Dylan songs I'd ever heard.

Folk singing I understood—hadn't I gone to hear the Kingston Trio in high school?—but Realpolitik meant nothing to me as yet (if it ever would). I'll never forget the image of a rather unworldly, eccentric professor of English—a noted scholar of Spenserian Neoplatonism and brilliant lecturer on Renaissance literature who'd taught me Shakespeare—emerge from the library into the bleak twilight of the scariest day of the Cuban missile crisis, listen silently to a few minutes of the back-and-forth Diag debate about the momently anticipated cataclysm, and walk off sadly shaking his head. There was obviously no place for nuclear war in his world of Ideal Forms. Nor in mine. While elsewhere on campus co-eds were picked up from dorms by their dads to be driven home to Kalamazoo or Grand Rapids for Doomsday, I spent the final hours of nervous indecision in sweaty argument with my downstairs neighbor, an eighteen-year-old Jewish prodigy from Horace Mann School, before word came through that the Russian ships had turned back. I can't remember the exact details of our disagreement now, except that it hinged on some obscure question of one's choice of logics for opposing war; as I recall, his reasoning was based on pacifist principles supported by citations from Gandhi, whereas mine was based on a desire not to be burned up, supported by citations from Beckett's *Watt*.

The denizens of the campus beatnik fringe, on the other hand, seemed way too cool ever to work up much of a sweat about political issues, or for that matter anything else—save possibly drugs, which they approached with a bizarre, exotic seriousness I found fascinating in a glass-bottom-boat sort of way. Wild tales circulated about beatnik naked parties, at which guests of both sexes were said to arrive wearing nothing but raincoats that were immediately removed, but I was never invited to one. A red-bearded renegade philosopher, rumored scion of old Prussian aristocracy and going by the name of Count Leopold von Bretzel, was bruited to be an organizer of naked parties at other people's houses. Once he intercepted me on the steps of a classroom building and attempted to sell me his tennis shoes for a dollar. Ratty, smelly and full of holes, these were shoes one would have paid good money to have removed from one's presence. Before this encounter, the last time I'd seen the Count—who often appeared somewhat less studiedly cool than many of the local hipster set, yet also quite a bit crazier—he'd been plunging through crowds of mystified sorority and fraternity types on South University Avenue, waving a fist in the air and chanting, "Human heads shrunk to the size of baseballs!" I was more than a little intimidated by him. I offered to purchase enough hamburger to make a meal for both of us, provided he would cease to wave his awful sneakers in my face. He accepted, threw them in a trash can, and accompanied me barefoot to my room, where I cooked the ground beef on my plug-in frying pan, and we ate it together in total silence. In his eyes I detected the sullen, remote contempt of the true beatnik, seeing right through me even as he gnawed on my meat.

Exile

After three years of increasingly intense and compulsive scholastic effort ultimately at the expense of all pretension to social existence, a degree with highest honors was awarded. Thus armed, one embarked on real life.

The first thought was to somehow cash in on all that work by turning it into freedom. The next thought was to leave the country. In 1963 I went abroad to "study," i.e., to learn to live. The generous proposal of a gentlemanly progress to a Harvard doctorate, by way of a Henry Fellowship, was passed over for a Fulbright to Cambridge because England spelled at once liberty and the past—that unlikely tandem of values which would in the long run provide the excuse for a cranky way of life, a turning both inward and backward, eventually to become the author's perverse distinction.

But just as I was so earnestly struggling to shed my national identity in order to become a citizen of the world, that identity sneakily reasserted itself. Passing by an out-of-focus television screen in the junior common room of a Cambridge college notable for its scientists and explorers, my new home in this first year abroad, my eye was caught by the image of an American naval ship at sea, as a news announcer reported its taking enemy fire in the Tonkin Gulf. In the months and years that followed, when fulsome, fatuous, Ugly American politician voices droned on promulgating the pressing of a war, I found myself hard put to listen. But the embarrassment of one's own real if involuntary sharing in that voice was inevitably to become a necessary self-chastisement. Not choosing sides in the conflict involved an almost impossible luxury of evasion in those years. I'm reminded of doing a magazine feature interview, some twenty years after his involvement in the war, with that disenchanted think-tank strategist, ex-military-advising circuit rider of the New Frontier, Daniel Ellsberg. My assumptions as to the naiveté of those who'd believed in the war in those early days were shaken somewhat when Ellsberg related to me the surprising depth of his initial commitment to the American cause, the practical application, as he explained it, of a high-minded ideal of scholar-warriorhood inherited from twentieth-century Western imperialism's most notable cockeyed-intellectual-ascetic-soldier-of-fortune-spook role model, T. E. Lawrence. Ellsberg showed me a photo of himself in Vietnam—a Harvard Ph.D. crouched in the elephant grass of the Delta, M-16 poking belligerently between tall reeds—then with his next breath wept over the enormous toll of human suffering in which the acting-out of his high Lawrencian ideals had implicated him.

Well, at least he'd believed in *something*. Having once waited hours through the northern night-frost for a chance to shake Jack Kennedy's hand in a college-town motorcade, perhaps I myself ought to have proven more loyal to that clever Irishman's war. Instead, avoiding both the commitment and the suffering, the cleansing with filth and the shame of the slaughter, at whatever sacrifice of career advantage, became a personal goal. Staying on in Europe represented in this respect an act of omission, more telling in terms of what I was *not* doing than of what I *was*.

Two years of fairly desultory scholarship at Cambridge were followed by two more years of same—accompanied by a little teaching work—at the then newly opened University of Essex, where I halfheartedly attempted to get a thesis on Ezra Pound off the ground.

What Lawrence of Arabia was to Dan Ellsberg, I suppose Ezra Pound was to me. While still at Cambridge, I'd used my first long vacation to set off in search of the sacred places of *The Cantos*, hitchhiking in Pound's long-cooled footsteps through the troubadour country of the South of France, at first dutifully, out of the simple loyalty of the pilgrim, but then with increasingly particular delight. After close encounters with Provençal landscape and Romanesque church architecture, I passed on into Italy to get next to the radiant stones of Venice and examine first-hand that Pound-proclaimed triumph of fifteenth-century paternalistic economics, Sigismondo Malatesta's glorious neo-pagan *duomo* at Rimini (where a joyless little curate inconveniently appropriated my passport, penalty for my trespass into a closed-off chapel to inspect Piero della Francesca's portrait of Malatesta). Finally I ascended the Dolomites into the alpine village of Merano in search of the Master himself.

Pound, I'd been told, was residing on a mountaintop above the town, at the familial castle of an Austrian baron who'd wed his daughter Mary. Armed with an ostensible "official" reason to visit, as the delegate of English art-collecting interests—I'd been appointed, in my innocence, to solicit the donation of the poet's collection of Gaudier-Brzeska sculptures to the Tate Gallery—I made the grueling hike up that sacred mountain, toiling sweatily past hefty vacationing Viennese in lederhosen and Tyrolean hats. My mission, though, proved fruitless. Leaning out a tower window, her striking high cheekbones remarkably evoking the leonine "Hieratic Head of E. P." carved from marble by Gaudier in London some half-century before and now planted on a slope in the castle garden whence its blind eyes stared up a spectacular valley between snowy peaks toward Innsbruck, the Baroness Mary de Rachewiltz informed me her father, no longer able to endure the chill of the brisk alpine nights, had gone off to Venice. As a reward for my persistence, however, I was asked in for tea. Suddenly embarrassed by my petty toe-in-the-door pretext of an errand, I downplayed the Tate solicitation as best I could; my hostess made it emphatically clear, once I'd got up the nerve to spill out my appointed purpose, that the English had never particularly endeared themselves to her father. What, she pointedly inquired, were the English prepared to pay in order to have what they were asking? Nothing at all, I was forced humbly to confess. My intended homage simply amounted to a fresh insult from a nation that had never really meant her father any good, any more for that matter than it had my own forefathers. This chastening conclusion to my trip contained a lesson I was as yet too young to understand, but appreciate in retrospect.

In and out of school poetry provided a life—of sorts. At a poetry festival in Bristol, Allen Ginsberg turned up unexpectedly, read a dolorous lament for Neal Cassady, then, when I stood up next to him in our little circle of poets to read, even more unexpectedly goosed me. He and I rode through the Somerset night in a motorcycle sidecar, me coming on about poetry, him just coming on. We hitchhiked together to Bath, then on to Glastonbury, where we visited the ruins of King Arthur's Avalon and Allen gleefully scandalized some old ladies in a tea shoppe. In open country miles west of Reading, rideless for hours as night and rain began to fall, I grew desperate, but an unfazed Allen calmly tried out his Buddhist hand signals, an alternative to thumbing that brought the next lorry driver screeching to a halt. This obliging Lancelot conducted us back to London. A few days later, with Ginsberg, Gregory Corso, Andrei Voznesensky, Diter Rot, Patrick Kavanagh, Robert Graves, Anselm Hollo, Christopher Logue, Harry Fainlight, Simon Vinkenoog, Adrian Mitchell and other poets of all nations, I participated in a "Wholly Communion" mega-reading at the Albert Hall. Dolled up like some wastrel son of Omar the tent-maker in a several-sizes-too-large mod leather jacket I'd purchased for three pounds earlier that day at a cut-price tailor's in the King's Road, I recited my poem "Superballs" and was heckled for my nasal Chicago accent by some wag in the third balcony.

The evening, like many spent in London's poetry *demimonde* of those years, segued into further confusions, reversals, adventures. I'd been camping across the river at the amazing Dickensian-dockside East End council-house digs of a young woman I'd met at a poetry festival in Nottingham, but at the Albert Hall found myself spontaneously befriended by a charming if rather fallen-looking duchess in a white vinyl minidress and shut-eye shades. She generously invited me back to her flat off the Fulham Road, and the next morning we staggered off on a bleary-eyed day trip to Winchester, a cathedral town of old buildings as beautiful as Oxford's or Cambridge's, but set among hills, trees, streams. Revived by the stroll past the west front of the cathedral, down College Street and through water meadows Keats had walked on another summer's day, I marveled at my poet's good fortune—then an hour later sank into deep gloom when it developed we'd missed the last bus to London, and had to thumb.

By and large life back at Cambridge left me feeling lonesome for my own kind, though there were happy discoveries of common ground with a couple of student poets who fancied the same kind of new verse I did. One was John Temple, a gentle, shambling undergraduate scholarship boy from the working classes up north. My first year at Gonville and Caius College, John dwelt in ground-floor rooms beneath my own in St. Michael's Court, adjacent to Trinity Church and the town market square. John became my best friend in college. He invested wistful yearnings for the American West in his poetry enthusiasm, and found in the lyricism of Edward Dorn, a maverick bard of those lonely western spaces he himself had never seen, the same purity of longing that he discovered in the poems of his fellow underclass countryman John Keats. Donald Davie, the lecturer in English who tutored us both in poetry, had alerted John and me to the articulate energy of syntax in verse; together quaffing congenial brews deep into the quiet college evenings, we earnestly compared the sinuous lines of Keats' *Hyperion* with those of Dorn's poems about that equally remote and mythy locale *Nyew* Mexico, as John pronounced it—to him an almost unimaginable paradise, to me, in my memory of my own youthful enthralled passage west at age thirteen with my grandfather, almost as fantastic. About all I could actually recall of New Mexico by then was my long-yearned-for first sighting of an actual mountain, the large, loaf-shaped mesa with a big white **T** on it at which I'd stared transfixed from the Cactus Motor Lodge in Tucumcari. Still, these pub talks of ours, continuing after closing time back in our rooms, often took on, as they advanced into the night, a curious tone of bittersweet sadness, almost as if we'd really experienced that wild locale whereof we spoke. In my new exile, I already found myself able to work up a powerful nostalgia for a homeland of big skies and painted canyons that never really had been mine, except through the same agency it had been my English friend's, i.e., that of a fanciful poetic imagination. Perhaps part of the appeal of such conversations lay in the peculiar exotic quality of lostness that places you've always desired take on for you when you begin to recognize they are getting farther and farther out of reach. Standing on Municipal Pier in Santa Monica drinking in my first awed sighting of the green Pacific in 1954, I'd developed my own individual fantasy of the West—about as unique as the banal longings of every other Irishman who'd ever left home to be burnt by an alien sun on that far shore.

A second Cambridge friend, Andrew Crozier, a diffident, earnest young Londoner, graduate of Dulwich School and at this time an undergraduate at Milton's college, Christ's, was a devotee of another American "outsider," the notoriously difficult Black Mountain master Charles Olson. Later, after both he and John Temple had put in time among Olson's little corps of disciples at Buffalo, Andrew joined me back in England as a grad student at Essex, where we reverently followed Olson's directive in plastering the recently-discovered Vinland map on the cover of the inaugural issue of a magazine we coedited, *The Wivenhoe Park Review*. (A chance to meet Olson himself on his November 1966 trip to England proved a surprising pleasure, the imposing behemoth of *The Maximus Poems* turning out to be a friendly giant who wanted to keep me up all night yakking about connective tissue and fish people from outer space.) Hearing of a budding poetry scene in the far north of England, Andrew and I hitchhiked together from Cambridge to Newcastle, a bleak, gray city then economically devastated by the decline of its traditional shipbuilding industry. There we found a little enclave of youthful working-class poets led by a dashing blond-mopped teenager named Tom Pickard, who on his minuscule weekly dole stipend was not only raising a family but running a poetry-reading series in the Morden Tower on the city's old medieval wall. (This enterprising youth had single-handedly spurred back into verse-writing the long-silent Basil Bunting, former Objectivist colleague of Pound and Louis Zukofsky and, though totally disregarded at that time, still one of England's finest living poets.) The lack of electric lights at our reading in the medieval tower was not for quaintness' sake but because impoverished young entrepreneur Pickard hadn't been able to foot the bill that month. We went ahead anyway with candles, and it felt like poetry was meant to be read that way. To college boys Andrew and me this trip was an altogether marvelous adventure. We were invited to read our poems on local television—certainly a first for both of us. We drank dark brown ale with young Geordi poets in Tyneside pubs rocking with a life and atmosphere that defied the gloom of the streets outside, and went dancing in a subterranean club filled by long-haired boys with the throbbing din of Marshall amps and flashing with the pulse of black-light strobes. This, too—so far from our world of Oxbridge and London—was England, perhaps much closer to the "real" England circa 1964.

Eric Burdon's then-popular song "We Gotta Get Out of This Place" made a particular kind of poetic sense in that context. Obvious differences in scale notwithstanding, the tiny underground poetry movement and the exploding electric rock minstrelsy of the period were essentially linked, the former as it were standing on the latter's shoulders; both constituted expressions of a generalized resistance against England's dead-end prospects. The Beatles and the Rolling Stones could still be heard in town dance-hall venues, as could up-and-coming mod bands like the Yardbirds, the Kinks, the Who and the Small Faces. Allegedly fueled by "diet pills" obtained from national health doctors by their dolly-girl consorts, young British musicians appeared to tap inexhaustible energy resources, memorizing their favorite R&B licks, distorting them into new dimensions and then playing them all night long.

Around this time a band of fairly typical going-nowhere Cambridge town kids, learning to play their instruments as they went along, started what in later years would have been called a "concept" band—if one can speak of calculated irrationalism as a concept—and began putting on England's first psychedelic light shows in a gloomy church hall near Notting Hill Gate in London. Pharmaceutical LSD was just then hitting England, and this band's shows at All Saints Hall amounted to unsolicited testimonials for it: prolonged baths in an acid ambiance still too inchoate to be a cliché, and not yet quite controllable enough to be successfully exploited (that phase wouldn't last long). Meanwhile their leader and guiding genius, Syd Barrett, zoomed through half-hour shoegazing guitar explorations on "Interstellar Overdrive," his signature composition, while bassist Roger Waters, a tall, expressionless zombie-type, lay prone on stage, staring up into the flashing cellular-blob projections as though mesmerized by a giant amoeba. Milling rather than dancing, we in the audience mimed the determined spaciness of the group, contributing our own semicomatose, vaguely participatory looniness to the occasion. One of my Essex students, also a Cambridge townie, showed me strange color drawings of cartoonoid hulk figures Syd Barrett had done on LSD. Later Barrett reportedly went off to India and "blew his mind" even beyond professional barriers. At Essex we still brought in the remnants of the band—Pink Floyd, they called themselves—to play for student dances. They'd learned to play their instruments, but without their certified-loony leader would never again be quite the same. It seemed true madness was after all not easy either to simulate or to survive.

 Another, tamer distraction from my nominal academic chores was my growing involvement with magazines both little and not-so-little. An opportunity to edit the poetry section of *The Paris Review*—arising out of an introduction supplied by my Ann Arbor teacher Donald Hall to that journal's editor, George Plimpton, who would prove a generously noninterfering if sometimes uncomprehending boss over the decade of my tenure—provided a pretext for contact with as well as occasion to promote the work of most of those contemporary poets I had latterly come to admire: both older ones (Olson, Dorn, Creeley, Ashbery, O'Hara, Schuyler, Duncan, Zukofsky, Whalen, et al.) and younger ones of my own generation (Berrigan, Padgett, Sanders, Saroyan, Coolidge, et al.).

Though at best only thirty to forty pages of poetry could be squeezed into any given issue of *The Paris Review*, before long I was swamped with at least five times that much interesting incoming material. The runoff, it soon became apparent, would require its own place. To the creation of such a place I devoted my nights at Essex, parlaying my own manic industry with the mechanical and postal resources of the university to crank out a dozen issues of a freewheeling, spur-of-the-moment giveaway mimeograph magazine, the "Once" series (O*nce*, T*wice*, T*hrice*, etc.). It went out to a mailing list of seventy-five to a hundred poet-friends on both sides of the Atlantic. Of the works to appear therein, perhaps the most notable in literary terms would be the seed-poem of the masterly mock-epic *Gunslinger*, whose author, the brilliant, craggy Ed Dorn, I had the good luck to befriend when he arrived at Essex as a visiting poet in September 1965. But immortal works were perhaps less to the point of the "Once" series than extremely transitory ones. The more-or-less instantaneous nature of the mimeo-mag project allowed it to keep up with an epoch whose essence seemed a Heraclitean flow: looking back now, much of what I published seems at once ephemeral and curiously indicant, a kind of unintended readout on times that were a-changin' faster than any culture that pretended to contain them. For example, in a brief poetic manifesto titled after his own folk-rock group, "The Fugs," New York peace-and-love activist Ed Sanders made a free-verse bow to the Rolling Stones, declaring their music "as important as the Magna Carta." The Stones LP Sanders singled out as news of the final tender human solution was the appropriately titled *Out of Our Heads*. Thought evidently had given up the ghost, now it all came down to bodies. Again, Ted Berrigan, another New York poet, to whom I'd mailed some mimeo stencils so that he could inscribe poems directly into my pages, sent back one stencil with just four words etched into it in huge block capitals beneath the heading "Poem for Ed Sanders": "I AIN'T GONNA DIE." An Immortality Ode for the new consciousness?

My strange nighttime office labors, though, once reported back by university porters, precipitated a moment-of-truth interview with my department boss, Donald Davie. My erstwhile Cambridge research sponsor, whose good graces were furthermore responsible for my position in this new program he'd come to head, Davie had by this time grown somewhat impatient with my failure to proceed in acceptable academic manner. Indeed, looking back, I think he had good reason to look askance: my penchant for guerilla publication was only the latest in a series of manifestations that also included my long hair, irregular period attire and evident preference for the company of my rock-and-rolling, hash-smoking students (as versus that of my Oxbridge-bred, pipe-smoking colleagues). Summoning me to his inner sanctum, he inquired sternly whether I intended to be a *scholar or a bohemian*?

Caught no more than a moment on the horns of that impossible dilemma, I abandoned my Ph.D. candidacy and teaching assistantship at the progressive university in Constable country. Cleaning out my bachelor digs in a quaint but bleak little North Sea fishing village, where the bemused gnomic eye of the Wittgenstein duck-rabbit figure I'd painted on the wallpaper to keep me company in my nocturnal poetry solitudes stared down upon two years of dirty laundry, I now had no job and virtually no assets save a somewhat battered trunkful of books and a steamship ticket for passage from Southampton to New York.

"White man, tomorrow you die"

"White man, tomorrow you die!" Ted Berrigan's *noir-humoresque* line had a prophetic half-life he couldn't have calculated when he applied it to his own little sphere of influence on Lower East Side streets. Passionate winds of the times blowing crossfire from several directions at once rang out their siren changes beneath the phrases of rock songs. History had caught a bunch of rootless, impoverished, footloose white kids confused and adrift at point blank range in its expiring backdraft. If it looked more certain every day that history in its received version might actually soon be *over*, there was equally little certainty as to what might be coming to replace it. In social terms especially this funny posthistorical vacancy was felt; in fact it sometimes seemed there was no class structure left at all. In terrain where the overlay of pot smoke and incense could neither eradicate nor mask for long those other odors in the grit-charged air—dread, adrenaline, amphetaminoid anxiety, rotten garbage, too-closely-packed, overheated human bodies—utopian collectivist philosophy just couldn't seem to take root, communal households inevitably devolving by stages into crash pads, then shooting galleries, then drifter graveyards. In the summer of '67, flowers and love settled

221

over San Francisco in a soft psychedelic storm, but on the streets of the East Village there lingered more than enough fear and resentment to go around. Here the period hippie tribalism of the West Coast would never really get off the ground.

My first month or so in the city was spent in an apartment on the nether reaches of East First Street, borrowed from the poet Dick Gallup. Dick and his family, out of money and plagued by a discouraging siege of robberies, had retreated home to Tulsa, Oklahoma for a few square meals and a respite from the trials of the city. The building was a testament to some unknown slumlord's legend. The graffiti-scrawled, piss-pooled, creaking, swaying ancient elevator was an adventure one wouldn't want to risk twice. Climbing the Raskolnikovian stairs, on the other hand, was not only depressing and exhausting but about as safe as a solo patrol in what weird-eyed street guys just back from Nam called Indian Country. Dick's place was on the third floor rear, with an exposed fire escape that offered perfect entry and exit routes for emergency "movers." During my stay, prospective burglars showed up every few days, peering over my shoulder past the chain lock to case the place, just on the chance a new TV set might have been brought in (no such luck). One particularly brazen prospector, a beat-up-looking guy in a big baggy overcoat, ogled the scene for a least a slow half-minute before remembering to pretend to explain to me what he'd come for. Producing from deep within his coat a balled-up out-of-date copy of *Muhammad Speaks*, he asked, "Want to buy a newspaper?" In fact I felt fairly invulnerable; the only vaguely stealable object I'd brought into the apartment was a vintage British-made Magnavox phonograph, but this machine, a big boxy white imitation-leather-covered console model, pawnshop value about five dollars, appeared hardly worth the trouble of any self-respecting burglar. I, however, valued it unduly highly. It was the shrine of that spaced-out Muse whose ghostly electrical visage, staring out from the museum of infinity, had kept me up past dawn spinning my half-dozen or so essential rock LPs for several years on sundry continents, and I didn't want to lose it (or them) now.

I went off to Chicago for a week, and left the apartment key with Ted Berrigan. On my return, I learned he'd left it in turn with a third party. When finally I retrieved the key and went to the apartment, I was startled to find both front door and fire-escape window gaping open, ancient Magnavox gone and my stash of precious albums vanished. My heart sank. I went over to Ted's to share my woes. It was late afternoon. A ray of sunlight slanted warmly from somewhere over by the East River into the tiny book-strewn front room. Ted was in a great mood, feet up on his desk, savoring the sugar rush of his second breakfast Pepsi, wagging his head from side to side in time with the rhythms of my Jefferson Airplane LP playing on the Magnavox. He'd come over to Dick's and picked it up to take care of it for me while I was away, he explained. Ted's social philosophy hinged on the adage, "Mi *casa, tu casa.*" What was his was yours, and what was yours was his. Living out his hero Kerouac's brave proposition—everything belongs to me because I'm poor—Ted was New York City's poet-realist answer to tribalism.

Eventually I found an apartment of my own, one tiny, tacky room on East Fourteenth Street near Avenue B. The sixty-dollar rent represented for me a princely sum, scraped together every month with no little difficulty out of my microscopic earnings from *The Paris Review* and from pickup labors like moving chairs around for poetry readings at St. Mark's Church—a fact which no doubt helped the place look better to me at the time than it does now in the mind's unsentimental eye. There was a hideaway bed that wouldn't hide properly (it had a "bent frame," handyman Ted astutely speculated), a dingy, unlit kitchen containing a cockroach watering hole of a sink and a minimal portable shower rigged precariously atop a cinder block that required a Right-Stuff-level sense of balance, a nonfunctioning turn-of-the-century brick fireplace containing a huge brass drum bearing the inscription of a Polish neighborhood social club, and some cast-iron-and-wire bookshelves found on the street. I lined the latter with books, which immediately accumulated a thick layer of dust and grime that sifted in through the barred but screenless windows from the Con Ed plant on the opposite bank of the turbulent traffic stream that was Fourteenth Street. (A decade later when Mount Saint Helens blew up and the volcanic dust-drift spread as far as Colorado, one morning surprisingly depositing a sudden grey residue on everything, the first image that flashed into mind was a recollection of that apartment.)

Across a deep dismal courtyard, there was a view down into a household of Hare Krishna freaks, who in the sweltering dog days of summer liked to hang out the windows in their gaudy, gauzy veils, no doubt half-asphyxiated by the steam of boiling rice stews, burning patchouli and sheer crush of physical overcrowding. Downstairs from me, a heavy covey of Puerto Rican junkies ruled the roost, up all night doing a serious trade in heroin and stolen goods, relentlessly playing the same Wes Montgomery track over and over at revving-jetliner volume on what had probably once been someone's very expensive stereo speakers. Paul Simon may have heard the sounds of silence echoing in tenement walls, but what I heard as I traveled up and down the vomit-coated staircases and landings of my building was a thunderous "A Day in the Life." This particular tenement was pressed smack up against a Chemical Bank whose power system hummed super-vibrantly all night long. I learned to live with my building's ambient noise, swallowed up in that general ungodly hum. Oddly, the daytime traffic racket on Fourteenth Street had a way of muting everything, like white noise.

Days were when I did my sleeping, anyway. One day I woke abruptly to the sensation of fluid dripping on my face from somewhere overhead. As there were several floors above me, rain would not explain this. Upstairs, a young unmarried mother who didn't speak English had broken a water pipe. I went up there, but could not explain the problem to her. The slumlord, a wizened old Russian, also pretended not to understand, until I threatened to withhold my rent payment.

The gentrification process that would turn these mean streets into a neighborhood where "nice" people lived wasn't yet so much as a gleam in a slumlord's eye. Beneath the thin surface veneer of hippie entrepreneurism—the sandwich stands, trendy boutiques and record shops—an indigenous domain still ominously remained, its lower depths cruised by potentially dangerous unfriendlies who dictated nervous rules of engagement, retreating into invisibility by day but, scary ghost-presences, emerging to rule the night.

After dark, not merely *where* you walked but *with whom* could quickly get to be a serious matter. After my first few months in town I ceased rambling the neighborhood at night with my otherwise good friend, the poet Michael Brownstein, who lived a block or two away. I couldn't help noting that Michael's particular sympathetic magic seemed to draw down upon us an inordinate share of street "bummers": having firecrackers thrown at us from tenement windows, being chased for blocks by crazed demanders of cigarettes, etc. My speculation was that Michael somehow brought these episodes upon us by neurotically anticipating them. For all I know, he may well have blamed them on *me*, and probably with equally good cause. Indeed it often seemed as though bad things happened to you in the streets in reverse proportion to your ability to handle them.

Foolish and intrepid in my long hair and Carnaby Street remnants, I must have shown up on those hostile street sensors as a perfect target. And with reason. Decked out in my purple Madras potato-dyed surgical attendant's jacket, I dropped in one day my first week in town to play my English Jimi Hendrix 45s for a Nigerian fellow I'd met at Cambridge, who was now living with Sun Ra's Solar Arkestra in a collective flat down around Third Street. Four bars of "Purple Haze" were enough to get me chased out, followed by ominous scowls, the double bolt slammed shut behind me. If I didn't know who I was, that didn't mean it wasn't visible to others. And in fact my nocturnal rambles of the neighborhood did not take long to pitch me into the clutches of troubles of all kinds. Mugged, bugged, ragged on and ripped off, I didn't require a microscope to get the joke. Territorial consciousness, developing almost overnight, suggested that finding a suitable hang-out partner was not just a good idea but an absolute imperative.

This need had a lot to do with the growth of my relationship with Ted Berrigan, which was in basic practical terms largely a matter of defensive strategy. Thinking back on it now, I'd moreover have to concede the strategy was probably one I'd learned long before, dealing with the minatory aspect of growing up on the West Side of Chicago, an environment in many ways unlike yet not always all that much kinder than this present one. My chosen best friend in grade school was the affable, burly captain of the football team, and in high school it was the six-foot-eleven-inch-tall basketball center. Having a large ally, I'd learned early, never hurt. Ted, for his part, was a fairly big guy who projected himself even larger; in the NBA they call this "playing big." Streetwise in summertime army fatigues or fur-lined Jim Bridger mountain-man cold-weather windbreaker, striding slightly bowlegged with arms swinging out at his sides in a sort of rolling sea captain's gait, the bluff, swaggering Providence Irish tough I found buried not too far under the skin in Ted brought out a goofy reckless Chicago Irish punk sidekick in me; wandering Alphabet City together, security actually seemed the least of our problems, well behind where to find, say, speed pills, danceable music, congenial friends, interesting books or free cookies.

    One night after a party at the Avenue D apartment of poet George Kimball, Ted had gone off in the opposite direction, toward Houston Street and home. Negotiating the bad stretch of Ninth Street between B and C at 2:30 in the morning, I paired up with Lewis Warsh, an angular, bespectacled, hypersensitive young poet from the Bronx. We hadn't ventured far when the "vibes," those all-sensing tutelary deities of the period, started to feel wrong; like shrinking walls in a nightmarish expressionist movie, the dark streets seemed to narrow in on us, looming up larger and larger as we ambled fake-casually along. Soon we had company: a quiver of slim shadows silently dividing off from the massed darkness of the other side of the street and gliding toward us with the unmistakable menacing purposiveness of serious misfortune incoming. We were trapped between our assailants and the parked cars that blocked off our route of flight. Honed-down blades of linoleum cutters pressed unsteadily against our throats, we surrendered our wallets. Watching my last forty dollars dissolve into the night, I choked back any useless—and possibly risky—protest. A tense eternity of five seconds or so went by, and then Lewis quite unexpectedly let out a strange, half-strangulated wail, clearly involuntary, somewhat resembling an animal's panic-stricken moan. It was a sound that could only have welled up from somewhere deep inside his trembling poet's soul. The tension broken, for his show of weakness Lewis was rewarded by having his glasses knocked to the pavement and stamped on. Tumbling in a pathetic cascade from curb to street, the broken pieces of plastic and glass added to the grit that was general all over our common world. For a moment the resonant echo of my friend's otherworldly howl of fear still hung in the concrete-encanyoned night. Standing in that echo I was as far from home as I'd ever been in my life, though still too young and foolish to understand it.

Uncloudy Day

In January 1968, I met my future wife, Angelica Heinegg, at an uptown party I attended with Lewis Warsh and Anne Waldman, who were acquaintances of the host. It was a party full of young short-haired stockbrokers. One of them asked sarcastically if I were "a member of the Byrds." My reply was to dance all evening with the prettiest girl in the room. Some weeks later this lovely young woman came along on a trip to Ann Arbor, where Ted Berrigan, Rod Padgett and I were all to read our poems as part of a week-long arts festival. We stayed in guest rooms in the Student Union. Angelica and I locked ourselves up in our room and acted like fiancés are supposed to. I remember Ted pounding on the door minutes before a scheduled poetry reading, loudly announcing, "You two are jeopardizing the future of American Poetry! Come out!"

Ted spent the days in Ann Arbor paying respectful homage to the ghost of Frank O'Hara, who'd written many of his early poems while in graduate school there. O'Hara had won a Hopwood Prize, as had I, Michigan in both his time and mine having been one of the few schools where a young writer could actually make a few dollars out of poetry. A memorial reading of Frank's poems took place—eerily for me—in what once had been the pool where I'd swum lonely college-boy laps, now filled in with concrete and serving as a Union lecture hall. Ron, Ted and I all took part; Ted's O'Hara reading was wistful and tremulous, and not without tears. One very cold day we all walked off campus to the rooming house on South University Street where Frank had lived. It looked like any other tree-lined street in Ann Arbor. We stood there shivering on the sidewalk, trying to share Ted's glow of holy-proximity-with-the-great. It was difficult. Ted was our Wordsworth and our Shelley rolled into one. No one else had that romantic sense of poetry's immortality.

Back in New York, store-window TV images on icy Second Avenue flickered a cold strobe vision of the present. At the end of the third week in January, *now* became a place in the middle of nowhere called Khe Sanh. TV showed us dark-green, brooding, mist-shrouded jungle-highland hills, red dirt, explosions, white smoke, blood, wrecked planes, wounded men, marines scrambling under mortar fire, close-in jet strikes, followed by the stock "Are you scared?" interviews—the shaking, exhausted boy-men in the bunkers, scared shitless, rocked out of their minds by an impossible history. A kid who'd played guard on my high school football team was there, trapped inside that ring of death. And where was I? I hardly knew, some nights, to be honest. Ten days later, on January 30, the Tet offensive hit network television. CBS showed the marine air base at Da Nang lit up by the impact of salvo upon salvo of rockets and heavy mortars, climaxed by a Fourth-of-July starburst of illumination when a storage depot took a direct hit and ignited chemicals and electrical supplies went up in towering flames. Angelica's twenty-fourth birthday fell a week after that, and we celebrated in my dingy hide-a-bed to the reverberating strains of the Staple Singers' *Uncloudy Day*.

In late March, we got married in St. Mark's Church. Two days before the wedding, while my fiancée and I were out securing a New York City marriage license, my apartment had been robbed and ransacked by the junkies downstairs. *A Day in the Life*. When I confronted them about this, they feigned remorse, but for the next two nights they kept climbing back up the fire escape to see if there was anything left to steal. It was time to go. After the wedding, I never went back to the apartment. I left what was there for the landlord to dispose of, and forfeited my deposit.

At the wedding, Ron was the best man, Ted gave away the bride. All three of us wore heavy wool double-breasted psychedelic gangster suits that looked like something left over from *Bonnie and Clyde*. These came from a poetry groupie named Shelley Lustig, whose husband ran a used clothing store. Not only were they similar to the outfits once worn by guys like Larry Fay and Frankie Marlow (from the Damon Runyon era), these may have been *the same suits!* Ted's was a grey three-piece pinstripe, worn over a dark blue shirt and white-and-green floral necktie. With his bushy reddish whiskers, this neighborhood Irish-American patriarch looked very colorful strolling up the aisle, the visionary bride in white lace on his arm. Poets David Shapiro, Dick Gallup, Larry Fagin, and the painter Mike Goldberg (who'd provided my Italian wedding shirt) played and sang the wedding music during the ceremony: "I Love You Truly." Afterwards, there was a party at Anne and Lewis's. In those moments when he wasn't busy kissing the bride, Ted proffered upon me solemn paternal advice on my new condition as a married man.

Jack of All Trades (Little Grub Street Testament)

> *In Liffey Street had furniture bugs and fleas I sold it,*
> *And at the Bank a big placard I often stood to hold it.*
> *In New Street I sold hay and straw and in Spitalfields made bacon,*
> *In Fishamble Street was at the grand old trade of basketmaking.*
> *In Summerhill a coachmaker, in Denzille Street a gilder,*
> *In Corn Street was a tanner, in Brunswick Street a builder,*
> *In High Street I sold hosiery, in Patrick Street sold all blades,*
> *So if you wish to know my name they call me Jack of all trades.*
>
> —Old Dublin Street Ballad

Once out of school there is the temptation never to look back: also the concurrent temptation never to look ahead. Almost-idyllic country-comfort family-founding years of a poet's life on a shoestring in a windy, eucalyptus-lit rural Pacific coastal hamlet called Bolinas—where, to paraphrase a poem by Robert Creeley, one of the many poet-friends who over the next decade would flock there, each day for all its flaws was as much as each wave washing up on that shore, perfect—dissolve in the late 1970s, as economic reality sets in, to relatively aimless wanderings wherever temporary employment beckons, from California to Colorado and back again, from west to east, east to west, south to north and north to south, subsisting day by day through a long contagion of free-lancing.

The man of letters who gives Grub Street as his address may wear his unprincipled professionalism as a badge of shame, but will not swear his allegiance till he cashes the check, his independence thus becoming a form of principle ironically doubled back upon itself. Implication follows hard upon implication: cumbrous months and years of a writing life all too rashly thrown into projects no more substantial than the wind, and all too frequently about as profitable. Executing literary labors assigned with variable degrees of attention by people one had for the most part never met, one found oneself doing many things one had never supposed the trade of literature might entail. The elements of surprise, challenge and adventure in these labors moreover before very long gave way to tedious sieges of oppression, tension and drudgery, interrupted now and then by outright catastrophe.

In these years I now speak of, I went everywhere I was told to go, read everything I was told to read, but didn't say everything I was told to say, and when questioned about it had only my own stubborn self-belief to fall back on as defense; and then that too fell away. I was edited to death, over the years, but each time like a phoenix staggered up from the ashes of my once-burnt-out, twice-shy sentences to be edited all over again. I learned eventually to expect that despite what was promised by those who'd put me to my toils, once the product was in their hands, the mail could be counted on almost never to contain the check. I'd once pretended to something more, but after a while I no longer recalled what.

Much though I professed to abhor it, however, this dubious business of free-lancing probably became me more than I was inclined to admit to myself. My character was always to betray my fate. I combined my father's self-destructiveness, artistic talents and dogged wrongheadedness with my grandfather's energy, though that also ran out after a while, and his good judgment I had always lacked. My affiliations were fierce, but unsoundly intense. I adopted groundless causes as though they were my long-lost offspring.

In this regard, the Grub Street pamphleteer-poet Tom Brown at times appeared to me in the light of a sort of perverse patron saint. Dean Swift once called Brown "the greatest genius of his age," by which he meant not the most delightful writer but the one most able to cause discomfort. Such gifts don't come cheap to the bearer. To chalk up to Tom Brown's influence the polemical pamphleteering of *The Great Naropa Poetry Wars* or *Stalin as Linguist*—to name the best-known of my Grub Street-style assaults on the pretensions of *soi-disant* literary avant gardes of my own age—would of course be stretching a point. Still, there *are* some telling parallels. Reckless habits of living paired with a certain defiance, which prevented his simply giving up, kept Tom Brown going, but his was a poor progress, ever deeper into debt. Recently an unsuspecting student inquired about the retirement plan at the fly-by-night institution where I have, for the past decade or so, supplemented meager free-lancing income by serving as a part-time teacher of literature. Images of a golden rope ladder gently descending from the sky, ready to pick one up, soon faded into a view of Tom Brown translated forcibly from his garret to the public sponging house. Grub Street has never had a retirement plan.

Epilogue: Poetry and Biography (Notes of a Lighthouse Keeper)

Is all true autobiographical writing in some sense elegiac? The subject is forever vanishing, lost like water seeping into sand as the wave retreats. Beneath the sand lie forgotten secret cities ... The work of a lifetime could be sunk into a self-excavation project such as this without ever getting to the bottom of it. To see oneself as others see one, let alone as one *is*—who's capable of that unimaginable feat? Perhaps it was when poised precariously at the brink of not only physical extinction but the further ignominy of eradication from human memory—forgetfulness, as each of us must instinctively suspect, is the *real* river of no return—that some saint or martyr once speculated that the power of self-knowledge would allow one to raise the dead. The ultimate eleventh-hour reprieve... But, upon further reflection, who'd really want to be the instrument of such fatal clarity?

    I recall the shock of seeing home videotape for the first time, walking with my friend the poet Aram Saroyan into an apartment in Cambridge, Massachusetts in the spring of 1967. It was the same week *Sergeant Pepper* came out; an amiable draft-dodger who was hiding out *chez* Aram kept playing "Lucy in the Sky with Diamonds," a supposed LSD anthem, over and over, but even that latest ratcheting of cogs in the cultural-consciousness loop had not prepared us. Entering that apartment in real time, we watched the previous moments played out by the inhabitants in a serial tableau incredibly unfolding before us. Presumably when *we* left, *our* presences, thus frozen into an instant past, would be equally so exposed. But watching oneself on videotape, what is it that one really sees—oneself, or the self one *was* a moment ago yet now no longer *is*, having shed it in passing like a snake's skin? Sex, lies and dreams...I think this amazing experience delighted Aram, whose avidity to participate in the brave new electronic world very much exceeded my own; I myself found it bewildering and disorienting. I've always been anxious to *get on with* time, and reluctant to go back to it.

Thus the present project's challenge for me: I confess the exercise of "telling" my life has proved difficult in the extreme. Everything connected with the concept of myself as a "public figure"—to start with—makes me terribly uneasy; of all one's several selves, that dwarf-grand "public" one must surely be the silliest, most insubstantial and deceiving. On the other hand, given you will never see yourself as you are, why deny the possible truth of that *other* you, which "others" think they see: your "identity" insofar as you have a name. Further, though, a name can go only just so far toward describing anyone. As the seventeenth-century poet Robert Herrick wrote in "Dreames,"

> Here we are all, by day: by night w'are hurl'd
> By dreames, each one, into a sev'rall world.

Not knowing oneself, when all's said and done, is a little like breathing, a habit one can give up only for a minute or two before serious consequences start to set in. Given *that* fact, imagine how uncomfortable things might quickly get if one were able to actually see one's various unidentical selves strutting their ridiculous pretensions to coherence through the eyes of others. Some levels of complication were probably meant to be borne only by language, in whose surprising reflections and sudden transparencies things take on for moments at a time a clarity that's spellbinding—or perhaps more accurately spellbreaking, shattering the data-hypnotized, stressed-out, hurry-up stupor of a life in a technologically administered society.

Within that society, to *be* oneself is almost too great a burden to bear; even, and maybe especially, in the chilling revelation of the lyric moment, the moment of negative capability when one's party to the projection of a kind of self-knowledge that's not individual but species-specific. As deep into the substratum of a collective life the undercurrent of our language seeps, the lyric never loses its power to follow, tapping the convergences of all those tributary streams, drawing off primary metaphors as trace elements from word roots. That underground current is the medium in which a submerged poetics can always be detected, rising back up to the surface like air bubbles behind a swimmer in water. Out of *mourning*'s unending pining history of sorrow and care, its riverine night of trembling and lamentation, reflective, mindful, unable ever to leave off remembering, the first faintly glowing buoyant light-geyser of *morning* again rises, abiding promise of mercy and forgetfulness, of a morrow beyond all compromise with death: the ultimate Irish wake.

Then again, there's nothing like the writing or reading of biographies to bring home to one the vanity and futility of individual human enterprise, and in particular of all attempt to discover in it some larger meaning or fulfillment, a role in some destiny greater than one's own minute, pathetically personalized private fate. The aphorist E. M. Cioran had it right when he suggested that every life is the story of a collapse. Heroes, villains, geniuses, achievers, cowards—all subjects of biography ultimately seem equally ridiculous in their obdurate failure to recognize the oblivion of their furious undertakings, that rushing toward a dead-heat last-place finish which sometimes seems the only thing that really involves one with one's fellows in the race.

Each clinging as best he or she can to a losing ticket, all winners have their distinct unlucky stars to thank for their particular negative triumphs. The prototypical story of a life in the capitalist petit-bourgeoisie, the East German writer Heiner Müller once suggested to me apropos a life of Céline I was trying to write, is that of a dog chasing its tail; the only story of the twentieth century to attain tragic dimension, that of the failure of communism. (Our conversation occurred seven or eight years back, when the collapse of communism still appeared to have some meaning beyond its invitation to intellectual despondency.) I think it was Heiner Müller's identification of the B-movie villain quality in Klaus Kinski—who at the time wanted to play Céline—that prompted these observations. But Kinski had learned the secret of overacting from his theater experience in the early years of his career. On stage, the futility of a life must be amplified to reach the back rows—what we now call the demographic bottom line. (Aim low, aim true, Céline once advised.)

The lyric poet, who is the playwright of the deepest and purest voices of the human collective's several selves, is briefly released from those selves' several internal conflicts by setting their baffling "characters" at each other's throats: his refusal of harmony while continually courting reconciliation is mimetic of the human struggle. What else are the figures of poetry but the extrapolations of all the continually collapsing lives that quarrel within us? These figures make it clear to us that a life's absence of meaning is finally the only reason to live. Such clarities, however, are once again not easy to bear. Burdensome as the writing of others' lives has increasingly become for me—after suffering through a half dozen or so of them, I've finally learned to give the whole business up—autobiography seems an even more acute kind of torment. Not knowing oneself is the universal law, Cioran also suggested, and no one transgresses it with impunity.

I've sometimes thought the most honest approach to autobiography might be the scattershot-schizoid "method" adopted by Rousseau in his *Dialogues*, a crazy conundrum of a work; though once conventionally regarded as at least semidemented, like some other historical works whose apparent evocations of madness have come later to possess for us a certain diachronic resonance, it now seems to have that quality we call "being ahead of its time." Rousseau's work is staged as a conversation of three voices, two of them variously identified with the author himself, the third that of an "impartial" outside observer. The mystery their extended conversation seeks to unravel is no less than the understanding of the author's life—and in particular of the disproportion between the "objective" literary value of his books and the bad reputation of their author. What makes this compelling text more than just the fascinating document of a hallucinated paranoia (it's also that, of course; Edmund Burke, who disliked everything about Rousseau, called it "the mad confession of his mad faults") is its curious verisimilitude, an almost uncanny truthfulness-to-life suggestive at once of mania and everyday reality. By splitting himself into three selves, each allowed only a partial knowledge, Rousseau re-creates those discrepancies of awareness which in real life separate not only the parts of one's selves but each person from any other. Much as persons fated to remain forever unreconciled—Rousseau's method implies—the quarreling simulacra of one's several selves may occasionally strike sparks that for a moment illuminate everything.

The late poet Jim Brodey was a particular friend of those "revolutionary" years when one's own sundry and various selves seemed conspiratorially shuffled every day like a deck of cards in the hands of some invisible dealer who had nothing to do with anything as coherent as Providence and everything to do with an intriguingly aleatory force of Chance. Back in 1967, he titled a book of his poems I*dentikit,* implicitly likening the reconstructive technique of the police composite image to the reconstruction of the authorial self in lyric poetry. The usual suspects, however, once released into the dispersive field of the lyric, seem to flee too quickly even for that kind of quasi-random identification. Autobiography would by that same trope be a way of rounding them up and bringing them in.

    The evidence of an old baby-book notation in which my mother comments that I seemed happiest when playing alone, the critical check marks against the column "works well with others" inscribed by concerned nuns in my elementary school report cards, and the fate of being a writer—what do these things have in common? To confess that one's often felt most comfortable with one's own company is certainly not a proud admission. Among trades with which this character defect is compatible, writing must rank right up there with lighthouse keeping. Solitaries apply. Rubbing up against one's own kind, anyway, has always seemed a pleasure more attractive in the being longed for than in the being gratified. Of course one's status as social animal justifiably suffers in ratio with the evidence of such a failure in natural sympathy. The ruined church of the old gods stands vacant on the wind-swept promontory watched over by the lonely lighthouse keeper, in his crabby, sullen art.

    Let's for the sake of the story place this lighthouse out in Dingle Bay, on the wild Kerry coast. Closing out a sixth decade on a loved, soon-to-be-lost planet, one inevitably tumbles into genealogy as into a grave one mistakes for home. "As we grow old we become more and more the stuff our forebears put into us," Willa Cather wrote in her tale "My Mortal Enemy." "We think we are so individual and so misunderstood when we are young; but the nature our strain of blood carries is inside there, waiting, like our skeleton." As if it were an x-ray of bones undergoing a shanty-Irish cell mutation, herewith our strain of blood offers you these notes.

Printed October 1995 in Santa Barbara &
Ann Arbor for the Black Sparrow Press by
Mackintosh Typography & Edwards Brothers, Inc.
Text set in Novarese by Words Worth.
Design by Barbara Martin.
This edition is published in paper wrappers;
there are 200 hardcover trade copies;
100 hardcover copies have been numbered
& signed by the author; & 26 lettered copies
have been handbound in boards by Earle Gray,
each with an original drawing by Tom Clark.

TOM CLARK was born (1941) and grew up on the West Side of Chicago. Of Irish ancestry, he was baptized Thomas Willard—Thomas after his maternal grandfather, a policeman, and Willard after his paternal grandfather, an itinerant sign painter. At St. Catherine's and Ascension parochial schools in Oak Park, he distinguished himself, according to rediscovered report cards, largely by his misconduct, although in 7th grade he earned first prize in the *Chicago Daily News* city-wide elementary school spelling bee. At Fenwick High School he became sports editor of the school paper, *The Wick*, while spending summers working as an usher at baseball games, horse races, prize fights and political conventions. Upon graduating from the University of Michigan in 1963, he attended Cambridge University on a Fulbright fellowship, and later did further research at the University of Essex—where he also began a marginal teaching career belatedly resumed, after some twenty years' interruption, in the 1980s. (Since 1987 he has been a member of the core faculty in Poetics at New College of California.) The intervening years found him taking up the doubtful trade of freelance writing, in which his labors have produced, along with a good deal of occasional journalism and criticism, a number of biographies cast in various forms: these include nonfictional accounts of the lives of writers such as Damon Runyon, Jack Kerouac and Charles Olson; "interactive" biographies of and with baseball pitcher Mark "The Bird" Fidrych and poet Robert Creeley; a historical novel about the exile of L.-F. Céline; and a verse novel, *Junkets on a Sad Planet*, based on the life of John Keats. He has also authored many books of poetry, including *Disordered Ideas*, *Fractured Karma*, and *Sleepwalker's Fate*. Married since 1968 to Angelica Heinegg, he is the father of a daughter, Juliet.